MODERN

RUSSIAN

TANKS

T-14

T-72

T-80

T-90M

T-72B

Other books we publish on Amazon.com

China Surface-to-Air Missile Systems

Customer reviews
★★★★⯪ 4.5 out of 5

Russia Surface-to-Air Missile Systems

Customer reviews
★★★★☆ 4 out of 5

GERMAN ARMORED VEHICLES

Illustrated

Customer reviews
★★★★★ 5 out of 5

NATO TANKS+

Illustrated

TR-85
T-84U
Strv 122B+
Abrams
Ariete
Leopard 2A6

Customer reviews
★★★★⯪ 4.6 out of 5

Modern Russian Tanks

By Alexandre Zanfirov

20 January 2023

I stand with Ukraine

DISCLAIMERS

The information and opinions contained in this document are provided "as is" and without any warranties or guarantees. Reference herein to any specific commercial products, process, or service by trade name, trademark, manufacturer, or otherwise does not constitute or imply its endorsement, recommendation, or favoring by the United States Government, and this guidance shall not be used for advertising or product endorsement purposes.

The statements of fact, opinion, or analysis expressed in this manuscript are those of the author and do not reflect the official policy or position of the Defense Intelligence Agency, the Department of Defense, or the U.S. Government. Review of the material does not imply DIA, DoD, or the U.S. Government endorsement of factual accuracy or opinion.

Preface

The Soviets (and now the Russians) produced so many variants of tanks (including for export) in the last fifty years that it would be impossible to include them all in one book. This book describes the major variants used by the Russian military and shows the distinguishing characteristics to make identification easier. Bear in mind that as time goes by, Russian designers continue to adapt existing tanks to increase lethality and improve survivability. So, some features seen on newer models are eventually incorporated on older tanks as a cost-saving strategy. Eventually however, modification of older tanks becomes uneconomical and a complete redesign is attempted. This is what we are seeing today with the advent of the Armata modular platform. In an effort to simplify production and reduce future costs, the Armata modular platform can accommodate multiple vehicle types with very little modification. It remains to be seen how successful this approach will be as manufacturing costs continue to inflate at a time when existing tank inventory still offers some life extension opportunities.

We added information on Russian tank company operations, tank maneuver instructions dictated under the "New Look" regulations as well as some lessons learned from the fighting in Georgia, Afghanistan and Ukraine. Some of these tanks appear truly formidable, however Ukrainian and Taliban Mujahideen knocked tanks out on a regular basis. It might take several RPG rounds, but they can be defeated. Perhaps that's why Russian regulars rely so heavily on infantry.

Due to the nature of "modern" explosive armor, it is not possible to fit every section of the tank with equal armor protection. If you have to face a modern Russian tank, the following spots of the tank (generally) should be targeted:
- the area directly below the driver's vision blocks (armor thickness reduced to make space for the driver)
- the lower front plate (no composite armor there)
- the gun mantlet and the area directly around it
- the sides and rear of the tank, as long as you are outside the frontal arc

April 23 UPDATE
I added 4 pages from a report written by Lester Grau titled "**Russian-Manufactured Armored Vehicle Vulnerability in Urban Combat: The Chechnya Experience.**" I wedged it in right after page 60. Basically it talks about the ways the Chechens were able to knock out Russian tanks and armored vehicles. The tactics they used were very effective at destroying or disabling Russian armor especially in an urban setting. The Chechens took advantage of some built-in vulnerabilities in Russian hardware they were very familiar with since most Chechens had served in the Russian military. Included are some diagrams showing the vulnerable locations of specific Russian armored vehicles.

Nov 12 2022 UPDATE
Added T-90MS Main Battle Tank as well as the alternate book cover.
Added examples of inflatable decoys of tanks and other hardware seen in Ukraine.

Jan 20 2023 UPDATE
Added T-90A showing 'coped cage'. This type of armor was proven ineffective and had little or no impact at all.

Alexandre Zanfirov
12 November 2022

Table of Contents

Russian Inflatable decoy tanks below.

T-72A Main Battle Tank (1979)

Widely considered as second-generation main battle tanks, the T-72 was an outgrowth of development of the troubled T-64. About 25,000 T-72 tanks have been built, and refurbishment has enabled many to remain in service for decades; production and development of the T-72 continues today. Initial production run began in 1972, a final trial batch was built as "Object 172M" and tested in 1973 and accepted into service as the T-72 in 1974. The original version was armed with a 125 mm *D-81TM* smoothbore tank gun. Historically, T-72 tanks had a slow reverse speed which prevented the tank from quickly withdrawing from a compromised position and performing an effective tactical retreat.

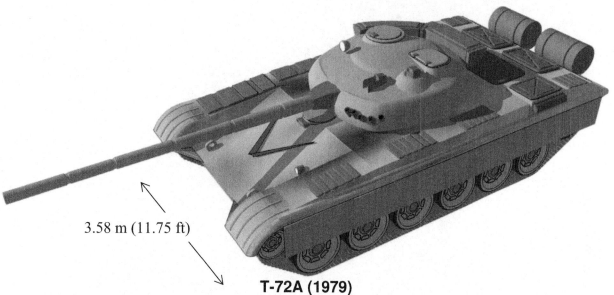

3.58 m (11.75 ft)

T-72A (1979)
Added laser rangefinder and electronic fire control, turret front and top being heavily reinforced with composite armor (nicknamed Dolly Parton by US intelligence), provisions for mounting reactive armor, smoke grenade launchers, flipper armor mount on front mudguards, internal changes.

2.19 m (7.18 ft)

6.91 m (22.67 ft)

Development continued in a series of block improvements. Obj. 174 introduced ceramic/steel laminate turret armor and the coincidence rangefinder was replaced with a laser rangefinder. Obj. 174 was designated as the T-74A when it entered production in 1978. Turret armor was greatly improved with Obj. 174M. A more powerful V-84 engine was introduced to offset the increased weight. Obj. 174M entered service in 1985 as the T-72B.

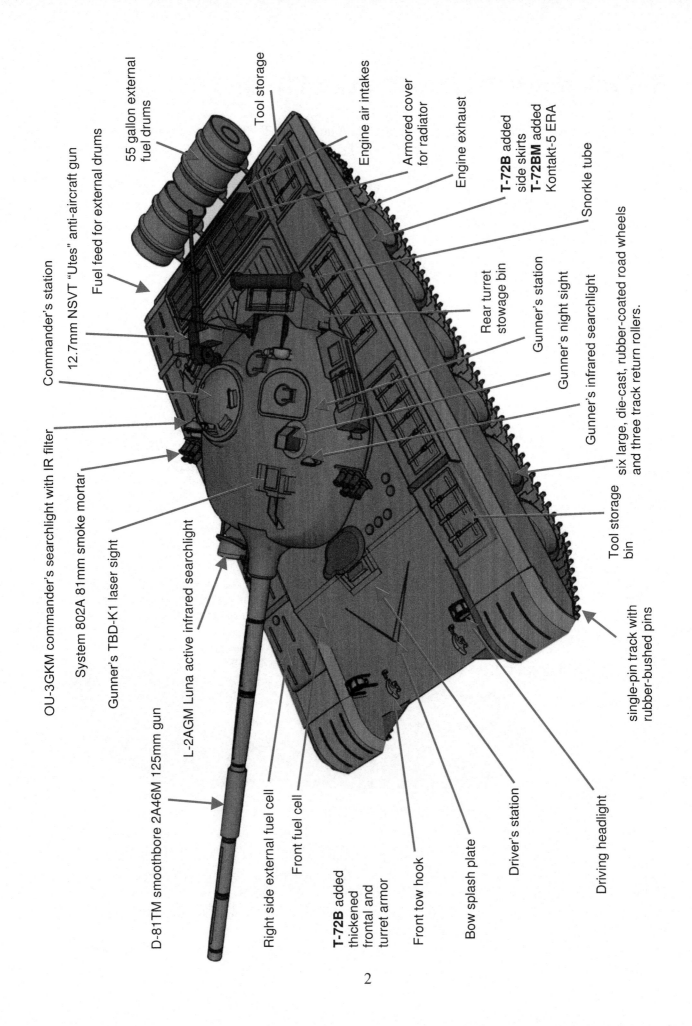

OU-3GKM commander's searchlight with IR filter

System 802A 81mm smoke mortar

Gunner's TBD-K1 laser sight

D-81TM smoothbore 2A46M 125mm gun

L-2AGM Luna active infrared searchlight

Right side external fuel cell

Front fuel cell

T-72B added thickened frontal and turret armor

Front tow hook

Bow splash plate

Driver's station

Driving headlight

Commander's station

12.7mm NSVT "Utes" anti-aircraft gun

Fuel feed for external drums

55 gallon external fuel drums

Tool storage

Engine air intakes

Armored cover for radiator

Engine exhaust

T-72B added side skirts

T-72BM added Kontakt-5 ERA

Snorkle tube

Rear turret stowage bin

Gunner's station

Gunner's night sight

Gunner's infrared searchlight

Tool storage bin

six large, die-cast, rubber-coated road wheels and three track return rollers.

single-pin track with rubber-bushed pins

T-72 Hull

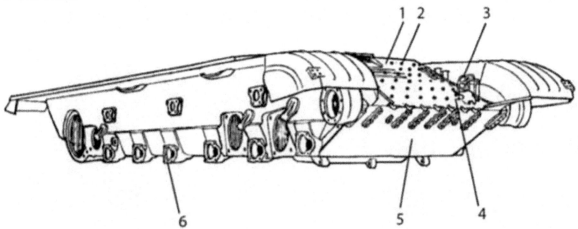

Hull. Front view on the right: 1 - leaf of nasal top; 2 – attachment lugs for installing DZ containers; 3 - headlight bracket guard; 4 – tow hook front; 5 - leaf of bow bottom; 6 - bracket balancer.

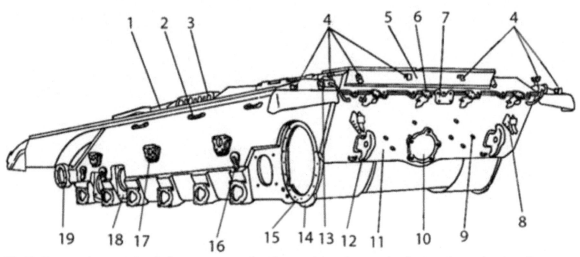

Hull. Rear view to the left: 1 - Protective bow plate; 2 - tracked tape; 3 - exhaust pipe; 4 - brackets and stops for stowing cables; 5 - beam with weekends; 6 - fuel barrel mounts; 7 - bracket fastening box of zip tray and PSK cassettes; 8 - log bracket fastenings; 9 - lugs for fastening spare tracks; 10 - fan hatch cover; 11 - leaf feed; 12 – tow hook; 13 - emergency socket case and overall lamp; 14 - chipper fingers caterpillar; 15 - Carter KP; 16 - balancing; 17 - bracket supporting rink; 18 - hydraulic reserves bracket; 19 - bracket crank wheels.

NOTE: The hull side, hull roof, hull belly and rear armor of all T-72 models are identical, regardless of the variant. The armor of the side of the hull is 80 mm thick. The armor on the sides of the engine compartment is 70 mm thick. There are several zones in the side of the hull that may not be entirely on the same thickness. The thickness of the steel armor at the drive sprocket (15) and the rear shock absorber is reduced (40 mm). It is thinner than the side armor of the engine compartment, and even though the shock absorber unit and the drive sprocket are backed by some amount of armor, the level of protection at these zones is not equal to the side of the engine compartment. The rear armor plate over the engine compartment is 40 mm thick, sloped at 30 degrees. The turret of the T-72 is generally tougher than the front hull armor because most hits land on the turret and not the hull during tank combat.

T-72 Turret

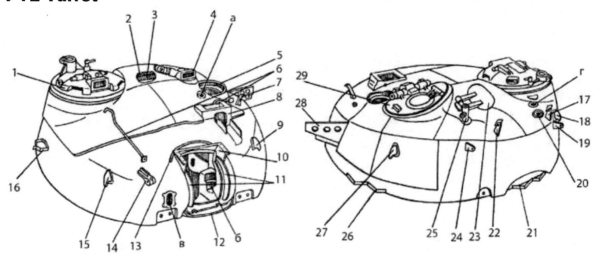

Turret: 1 - turret commander; 2 - copiers; 3 - roof; 4 - body to install a meter surveillance device; 5 - flange for installation of the sight 1K13-49; 6 - tubes for electrical wires; 7, 25 - headlight mount brackets; 8 - sight-rangefinder; 9, 15, 18, 27- hook assembly; 10 - bracket; 11 - gun arc brackets; 12, 13 brackets for fastening the outer protective cover (mask) of the gun; 14 - the bracket of the L-4A searchlight; 16-clamp fastening box with ammunition for machine gun NSV; 17, 19, 22, 24 - brackets fastening of the boxes of the ODLT; 20 - antenna fastening flange; 21, 26 - copiers; 23 - hatch vent and removal of the pallet; 28 - bracket for smoke grenade launchers; 29 - gunner viewer.

Fuel Supply System

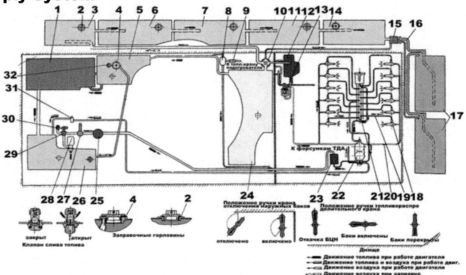

Fuel supply system: 1- right nose tank; 2.4- filling neck; 3, 6, 7, 11, 14 - exterior tanks; 5 - front tank rack; 8 - heater fuel pump; 9 - fuel filter heater; 10 - shutdown of external tanks; 12 - expansion tank; 13 - float valve; 15 - adapter for connecting barrels; 16 - equipment for connecting barrels; 17 - barrels; 18 - nozzle; 19 - high pressure pipeline; 20 - pipeline of combined fuel pump from nozzles; 21 - NK-12M fuel pump; 22 - fuel filter fine cleaning; 23 - to-fuel pump NTP-46; 24 - medium tank rack; 25 - fuel filter coarse cleaning; 26 - left nose tank; 27 - manual fuel pump; 28 - fuel pump BTSN-1; 29 - fuel distribution valve; 30 - drain fitting; 31 - air release valve; 32, 36 - hoses; 33 - socket; 34 - pump sludge; 35 - tee; 37 - fuel meter.

T-72 125mm Smoothbore Gun

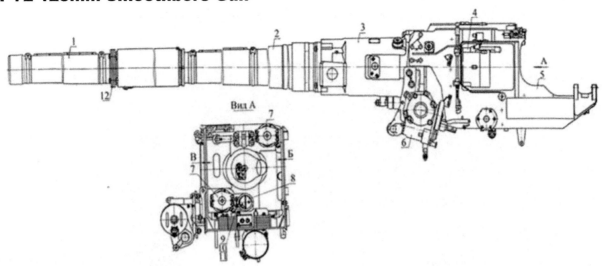

Tank gun 2A46m: 1 - thermal protective cover; 2 - trunk; 3 - cradle; 4 - shutter; 5 - fence; 6 - lifting mechanism; 7 - brake of retractable parts; 8 - aperture; 9 - bracket; 10 - screw; 11 - wire; 12 - compensating cargo; Б - gap 8-13 mm; В - gap 8-12 mm.

7.62mm Anti-aircraft Machine Gun

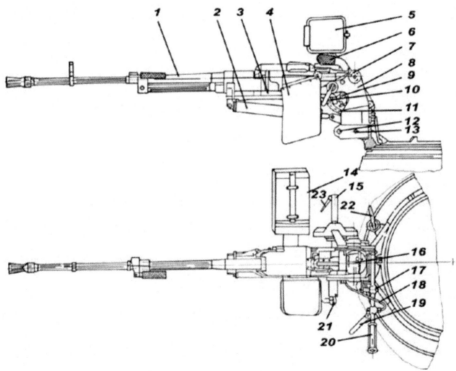

Anti-aircraft machine gun: 1 - machine gun NSV-12.7; 2 - balancing mechanism; 3 - Lulka; 4 - tape collector; 5 - sight; 6 - handle machine gun platoon; 7 - pin; 8 - plug; 9 - machine check; 10 - Spring Range; 11 - toothed sector of the cradle; 12 - the clamping screw of the hatch socket; 13 - fixation bolt plugs in the nest; 14 - store for cartridges; 15 vertical guidance; 16 - machine gun descending; 17 - stopper handle; 18 - cable; 19 - machine gun descent; 20 - horizontal guidance handle; 21 - stopper cradle; 22 - middle pursuit stop; 23 - flywheel brake key.

T-72 Armor Vulnerabilities

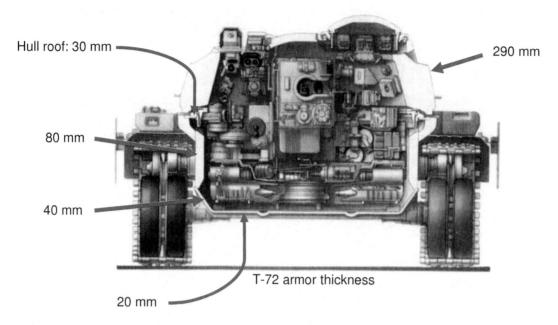

Hull roof: 30 mm

290 mm

80 mm

40 mm

20 mm

T-72 armor thickness

The turret of the T-72 is a very, very tough nut to crack from a wide range of angles. The unique teardrop shape of the turret makes it possible to present a high thickness of armor across the frontal arc. However, this shape does not come without drawbacks. It is extremely efficient in the distribution of armor mass because it can provide a very high level of protection in its frontal arc with comparatively little armor compared to heavier turrets, but because the vast majority of the mass is disproportionately allocated to the front, the turret became unbalanced. A balanced turret generates a more stable load on the stabilizer, making it easier to implement faster and more precise turret rotation drives, and it also reduces the stress on the turret ring from firing the main gun at various gun elevation angles and at various tank orientation angles. The turret of a basic T-72A weighs 12 tons (including the weapons and a full set of standard equipment) and its center of gravity is 500 mm above the level of the turret ring race ring and horizontally offset 430 mm from the geometric center of the turret ring. The turret of the T-72B has even heavier frontal armor and is even more unbalanced, and the addition of explosive reactive armor on the frontal arc exacerbates the issue.

Commander's cupola: The commander's cupola is a weakened zone that extends above the turret roof and cannot be armored as thickly as the rest of the turret.

Driver's periscope area: The weakened zone at the driver's periscope is created by the void in the upper glacis necessitated by the installation of the driver's periscope as well as the need to accommodate the driver's head.

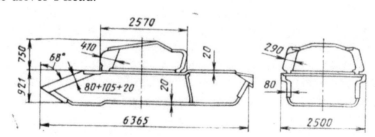

Рис. 3.8. Схема броневой защиты танка Т-72

6

Specifications (T-72A)

Mass	41.5 tons (45.7 short tons),
	44.5 tons (49.1 short tons) (**T-72B**)
Length	9.53 m (31 ft 3 in) gun forward
	6.95 m (22 ft 10 in) hull
Width	3.59 m (11 ft 9 in)
Height	2.23 m (7 ft 4 in)
Crew	3 (commander, gunner, driver)
Armor	Steel and composite armor with ERA
Main armament	125 mm D-81TM smoothbore gun (**T-72 1974**)
	125 mm 2A46M/2A46M-5 smoothbore gun (**T-72A 1979**)
Secondary armament	7.62 mm PKT coax. machine gun
	12.7 mm NSVT or DShK anti-aircraft machine gun
Engine	V-12 diesel
	V-92S2F (**T-72B3 & T-72B3M**)
	780 hp (580 kW)
	1,130 hp (840 kW) for V-92S2F
Power/weight	18.8 hp/ton (14 kW/ton)
Transmission	Synchromesh, hydraulic assist with 7 forward and 1 reverse gear
Suspension	Torsion bar
Ground clearance	0.49 m (19 in)
Fuel capacity	1,200 L (320 U.S. gal; 260 imp gal)
Operational range	460 km (290 mi), 700 km (430 mi) with fuel drums
Max speed	60 to 75 km/h (37 to 47 mph)

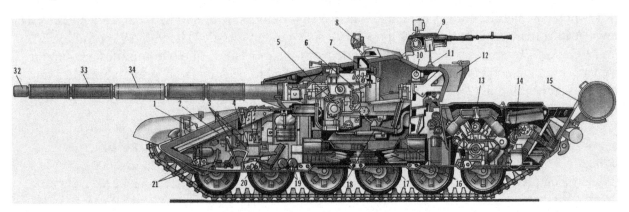

T-72K

The T-72K is the command version of T-72 with an additional R-130M radio. Company command versions were fitted with two R123M/R-173 additional radios and also carried a 10 m telescopic mast. Battalion and regiment command versions were fitted with two R123M/R-173 additional radios and the R-130M that uses the 10 m mast when its erected. In NATO code T-72K was represented by three different designations: T-72K1, T-72K2 and T-72K3 which represented the company command version, battalion command version and regiment command version.

T-72B Main Battle Tank (1985)

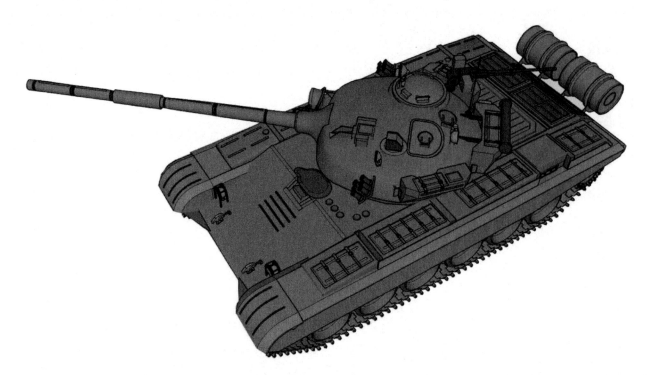

The T-72B (NATO code: SMT M1988) was a much-improved version with 1A40-1 fire control system, thicker armor, turret front and top was heavily reinforced with composite armor better known by its US codename "Super Dolly Parton", 20 mm of appliqué armor in the front of hull, 1K13-49 sight, stabilization system, and a new V-84-1 engine with 840 hp (626 kW). Received a new 2A46M main gun capable of firing *9M119 Svir* guided missile. The 9M119 Svir and *9M119M Refleks* are laser beam riding, guided anti-tank missiles. The two missiles are similar, but vary in range and launch platform. Both are designed to be fired from smooth bore 125 mm tank and anti-tank gun (2A45, 2A46 and 2A46M). Their NATO reporting name is AT-11 Sniper. The name Svir comes from the River Svir, while Refleks means reflex.

	Svir	Refleks
Range	75 to 4,000 m	75 to 5,000 m
Weight (complete round):	28 kg	24.3 kg
Missile Weight:	16.5 kg	17.2 kg
Warhead:	Tandem HEAT	
Penetration:	700–900 mm (35.4 inches) of RHA	
Time of flight to 4,000 m:	11.7 s	
Time of flight to 5,000 m:		17.6 s

T-72BA ERA

Fitted with 227 "Kontakt-1" ERA bricks to the hull and turret. The glacis plate and turret is covered with a layer of single ERA blocks and the turret's bottom row is mounted horizontally. There's also an ERA array on the side skirts. The driver's seat is now suspended from the ceiling instead of being fixed to the floor and the driver's station has a new steering system as well as a new TVN-5 night sight. Has newly developed twin-pin tracks.

T-72B3 model 2011 (~2010)

Upgrade for T-72B tanks, including Sosna-U multichannel gunner's sight, new digital VHF radio, improved autoloader, 2A46M-5 gun to accommodate new ammunition. Retains older V-84-1 840 hp (630 kW) engine and second-generation **Kontakt-5 explosive reactive armor**, and lacks satellite navigation.

Multichannel thermal imaging sighting device gunner "Sosna-U"
TPV Sosna-U was developed by Belarusian designers of the Peleng enterprise (Minsk). However, the sight is produced in Russia by the Vologda enterprise VOMZ.

The main characteristics of TPV "**Sosna-U**"
- optical day channel
- thermal imaging channel, which uses a second-generation thermal imaging camera with 8–12-micron characteristics
- laser range finder;
- channel to control missiles
- distance to 5 kilometers of detection of objects of the class "tank"
- independent 2-x planar stabilization

Kontakt-5 explosive reactive armor (ERA)
Conventional ERAs are capable of defeating shaped-charge jets, Kontakt-5 can also defeat APFSDS rounds. Because of Kontakt-5, long-rod penetrators can lose over 30% of their penetration potential and the protected vehicle becomes immune to them. While light ERA containers are completely destroyed in the process of detonation, Kontakt-5 sections are not, as their detonation is contained by the outside armor plates. The Ukrainian Army reported success using teams of tanks to destroy Russian T-72B3 tanks on several occasions, but multiple hits were required to defeat the T-72B3's second-generation Kontakt-5 explosive reactive armor.

T-72B3M model 2016 (2014)

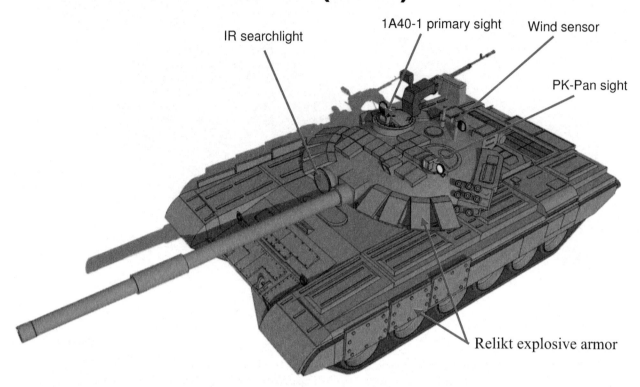

IR searchlight

1A40-1 primary sight

Wind sensor

PK-Pan sight

Relikt explosive armor

The T-72B3M, also referred to (incorrectly) as T-72B4, is an upgraded variant of the T-72B3. The tank features an advanced fire control system and a new thermal sight. The T-72B3M tank is equipped with radio systems for encrypted digital voice and data transfer, snorkels for deep fording, a built-in blade for self-entrenching and increased protection against mines. The T72B3M is armed with a **2A46M5 125 mm** smoothbore gun loaded by an auto-loader that can fire advanced projectiles: high-explosive fragmentation (HEF) and high-explosive anti-tank (HEAT), armor-piercing discarding sabot (APDS) as well as 9M119M Refleks (NATO codename: AT-11 Sniper) guided anti-tank missiles.

The AT-11 Sniper missile has a maximum range of 4 km and can engage tanks fitted with explosive reactive armor. The secondary armament includes a co-axial 7.62 mm PKTM machine gun and a roof-mounted 12.7 mm NSV heavy machine gun. The turret has eight smoke grenade launchers and a wind sensor.

The T-72B3M tank commander has a new panoramic PK PAN sight with thermal vision. The sight includes a day channel, a laser range finder and an image intensifier to search for targets and assign them to the gunner and direct the turret. The fire control system is interfaced with sighting system and a ballistic computer. The T-72B3M MBT is equipped with the new **Relikt** explosive reactive armor (ERA) that provides superior protection against shaped charges, tandem warheads, APFSDS rounds and anti-tank guided missiles.

The B3 upgrade includes a new explosion and fire suppression system, as well as an advanced VHF radio system designated R-168-25U-2 AKVEDUK.

T-72BM Cutaway

Other books we publish on Amazon.com

Russia Land-Based Electronic Warfare/RUMINT

Customer reviews
★★★★☆ 4 out of 5

CHINA ELECTRONIC WARFARE WEAPONS/ RUMINT

Customer reviews
★★★★☆ 4 out of 5

CHINA MRAPs, ARMORED CARS, ARMORED PERSONNEL CARRIERS & ARMORED ASSAULT VEHICLES

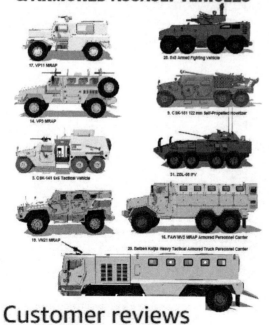

Customer reviews
★★★★★ 5 out of 5

RUSSIA MRAPs, ARMORED CARS, ARMORED PERSONNEL CARRIERS & ARMORED ASSAULT VEHICLES

Customer reviews
★★★★★ 5 out of 5

T-80 Main Battle Tank (1976)

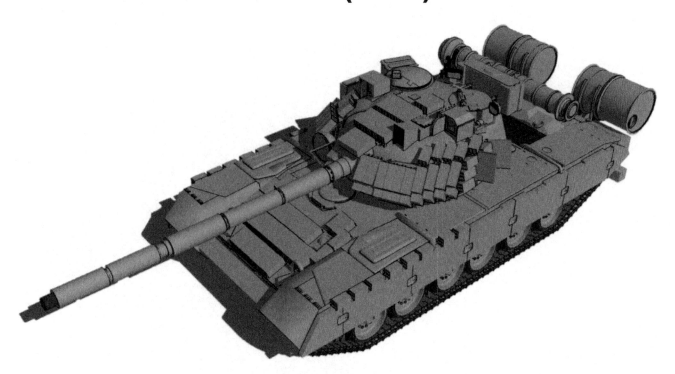

The T-80 is based on the T-64, while incorporating features from the later T-72. The T-72 and T-80 look alike but are mechanically very different. The T-72 is mechanically simpler, easier to manufacture, and easier to service in the field. When the T-80 entered service in 1976, it was equipped with a gas turbine engine as primary propulsion, some later variants reverted to a diesel engine because the gas turbine consumed fuel rapidly, even at engine idle. Russia operates a total of 4,500 T-80 main battle tanks of all variants. The glacis is of laminate armor and the turret is armored steel, with cavities in the turret cheeks containing either a ceramic filling or non-explosive reactive armor elements. The turret houses the same 125 mm 2A46 smoothbore gun as the T-72, which can fire anti-tank guided missiles as well as regular ordnance. The tracks are slightly wider and longer than on the T-64 giving lower ground pressure. The main gun is fed by the *Korzina automatic loader*. This holds up to 28 rounds of two-part ammunition in a carousel located under the turret floor. The autoloader takes between 7.1 and 19.5 seconds to load the main weapon. The propellant charge is held inside a semi-combustible cartridge case made of a highly flammable material – this is consumed in the breech during firing, except for a small metal baseplate.

The T-80BV variant was vulnerable to catastrophic explosion because of the stored semi-combustible propellant charges and missiles when contacted by the molten metal jet from the penetration of a HEAT warhead, causing the entire ammunition load to explode. The T-80's first (and only) use in combat was in 1994 in the First Chechen War, where they suffered heavy losses in urban combat. Due to design flaws and high operating costs, Russia has not used the tanks in later conflicts such as the 1999 Second Chechen War, the 2008 Russo-Georgian War, or the 2014 Russo-Ukrainian War.

T-80B / T-80U Specifications

Mass	42.5 tons T-80B, 46 tons T-80U
Length	9.9 m (32 ft 6 in) T-80B, 9.654 m (31 ft 8.1 in) T-80U (gun forward) 7.4 m (24 ft 3 in) T-80B, 7 m (23 ft 0 in) T-80U, (hull)
Width	3.4 m (11 ft 2 in) T-80B 3.603 m (11 ft 9.9 in) T-80U
Height	2.202 m (7 ft 2.7 in) T-80B, T-80U
Crew	3
Armor	
T-80B –	Hull 440–450 mm vs APFSDS 500–575 mm vs HEAT, Turret 500 mm vs APFSDS, 650 mm vs HEAT
T-80U –	Hull & Turret with Kontakt-5 780 mm vs APFSDS 1,320 mm vs HEAT

Main armament	125 mm 2A46-2 smoothbore gun, 36 rounds T-80B, 2A46M-1 with 45 rounds T-80U; 9M112 Kobra ATGM, 4 missiles T-80B, 9M119 Refleks ATGM, 6 missiles T-80U
Secondary armament	7.62 mm PKT coax MG, 12.7 mm NSVT or DShK or PKT antiaircraft MG
Engine	SG-1000 gas turbine T-80 GTD-1250 turbine; or one of 3 diesel engines - T-80B 1,000 hp, T-80U 1,250 hp, T-80UD 1,000-hp 6TD engine
Power/weight	23.5 hp (17.6 kW) / ton T-80B; 27.2 hp (20.3 kW) / ton T-80U
Transmission	Manual, 5 forward gears, 1 reverse T-80B, 4 forward, 1 reverse T-80U
Suspension	Torsion bar
Gnd clearance	0.38 m (1.2 ft) T-80B, 0.446 m (1.46 ft) T-80U
Fuel capacity	1,100 liters (240 imp gal) (internal) 740 liters (160 imp gal) (external)
Operational range	335 km (208 mi) (road, without external tanks) 415 km (258 mi) (road, with external tanks)
Max. speed	80 km/h (50 mph) (T-80U, road) 48 km/h (30 mph) (cross country)

Russian T-80U of the 4th Tank Brigade, 2011.

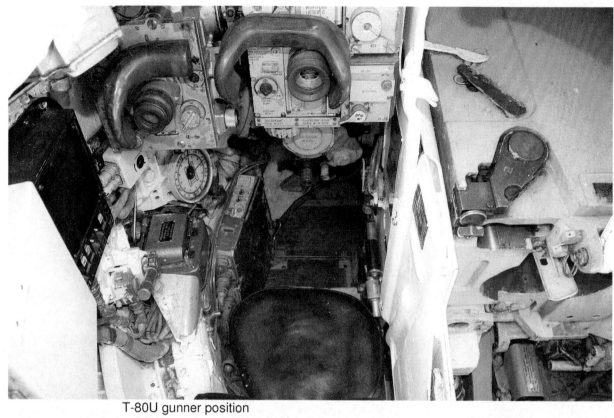

T-80U gunner position

T-80U commander position

T-80BVM Main Battle Tank (2017)

Installed "Relikt" ERA, PNM Sosna-U gunner sight (as in the T-90, T-72B3), the improved 125mm gun 2A46M-4, the upgraded gas turbine engine and the upgrades of various other systems. The Russian armed forces have received all the modernized T-80BVM tanks under the contract with the Rostec corporation, signed in 2017, Rostec said on 12 December 2019. A new contract for 50 tanks was signed in August 2020.

This T-80BV has reactive armor adapted to its turret and hull.

Inflatable T-80 tank decoy.
Note the compressor at top right
and power cord for the thermal
elements sewn into the fabric.

T-90 Main Battle Tank (1992)

The third-generation Russian main battle tank entered service in 1993. It is a modern variation of the T-72B and incorporates many features found on the T-80U. Russia operates 369 T-90A, 120 T-90 and 38+ T-90M tanks. There are an estimated 5,200 T-90 Series tanks in storage. The principal upgrade in the T-90 was the incorporation of a slightly modified form of the T-80U's more sophisticated 1A45T Irtysh fire control system and an upgraded V-84MS multi-fuel engine developing 830 hp (620 kW).

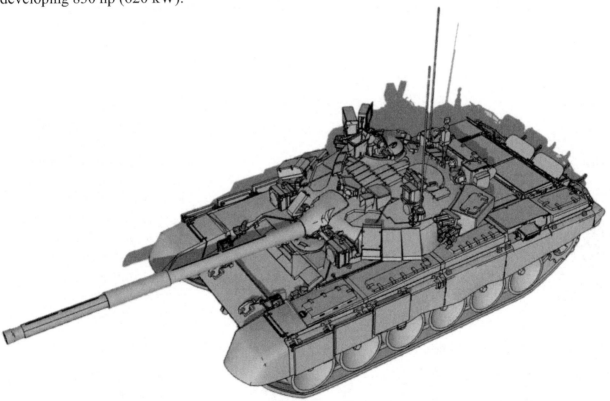

Various T-90 Turrets

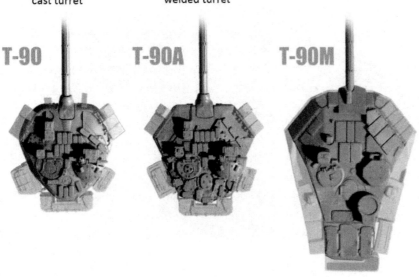

T-90

T-90A

cast turret

welded turret

T-90   **T-90A**   **T-90M**

TShU-1-7 Shtora-1 EOCMDAS

The Shtora-1 EOCMDAS (electro-optical counter-measures defensive aids suite) is designed to protect against the two most common ATGW types: wire-guided SACLOS systems (e.g. TOW, HOT) and laser-guided ATGMs (e.g. Hellfire, Copperhead). Shtora-1 consists of a specialized computer/control panel, two electro-optical interference emitters located on each side of the gun, four laser sensors located on top of the turret, and racks of dedicated anti-laser smoke grenades. For the TOW missile, the emitters create a large hotspot, essentially tricking the missile guidance into following the Shtora hotspot instead of the missile's flare hotspot, resulting in faulty course corrections by the ATGW computer.

When a laser beam is detected, the Shtora informs the crew with light and sound; it then launches laser defeating smoke grenades, that enshroud the tank and break or degrade the lock. Tank commander can also press a button that will turn the turret front to the laser to meet incoming ATGM with the best protected section and to engage the laser beam source with the maingun.

20

T-90A Main Battle Tank (2005)

The T-90A is an improved Russian army version with welded turret, V-92S2 engine and ESSA thermal viewer. Early T-90A tanks were powered by the V-92S2 engine, carried a T01-K05 Buran-M gunner's sight (passive-active night-vision channel with an EPM-59G Mirage-K matrix and a maximum observation distance of 1,800 m) and were protected by the most recent Kontakt-5 explosive reactive armor with 4S22 explosive tiles. Starting in 2006, T-90A tanks were fitted with entirely passive ESSA main gunner's sights supplied by Peleng in Belarus and using the 2nd-generation thermal camera Catherine-FC from Thales, as well as improved 4S23 ERA tiles. The Catherine-FC thermal imaging devices were used to develop "ESSA", "PLISA" and "SOSNA-U" sighting systems.

T-90A with Coped Cage

Cope cages began appearing on top of armored vehicles during the Russian invasion of Ukraine (2022). With the introduction of the NATO **FGM-148 Javelin Anti-Tank Missile** in the battlefield, Russian forces attempted to counter them by adding improvised steel grilles known as 'cope cages'. This overhead slat armor was meant to take the impact of the missiles on the account that most would be hitting the turret of the tank where the armour is the weakest. This type of armor was proven ineffective and had little or no impact at all.

T-90AM Proryv-2 Main Battle Tank

The T-90AM (Object 188AM) was a project to modernize the T-90A. A new automatic loader and an upgraded 2A46M-5 cannon were installed, as well as a remotely controlled 7.62-mm anti-aircraft gun "UDP T05BV-1." New engine and automatic transmission V-92S2F with 1130 hp. The exhaust system is located in the fenders to reduce the hull temperature and the tank's visibility for IR guidance systems. A new engine is installed in a single unified unit with an automatic transmission. A new turret was installed, equipped with the "*Kalina*" fire control system with an integrated combat information and control system. The commander's panoramic sight contains a two-plane independent stabilization for view of the battlefield, new laser rangefinder, television and thermal imaging channels. Installed the multi-channel sight of the operator-gunner "*Sosna-U*." Only the T-90AM has an *active protection system (APS)*. It partially uses elements of the "*Afghanit*" active protection complex found on the Armata T-14 tank.

An active protection system is designed to prevent anti-tank missiles/projectiles from acquiring and/or destroying a target. **Electronic countermeasures** that alter the electromagnetic, acoustic or other signatures of a target thereby altering the tracking and sensing behavior of an incoming threat (e.g., guided missile) **are designated soft-kill measures**. Measures that **physical**ly counterattack an incoming threat thereby destroying/altering its payload/warhead in such a way that the intended effect on the target is severely impeded **are designated hard-kill measures**.

The Afghanit (Russian: Афганит) active protection system, which includes a millimeter-wavelength radar to detect, track, and intercept incoming anti-tank munitions, both kinetic energy penetrators (reportedly) and tandem-charges. Currently, the maximum speed of an intercepted target is 1,700 m/s (Mach 5.0), with projected future increases of up to 3,000 m/s (Mach 8.8). According to news sources, it protects the tank from all sides.

Afghanit hardkill (red) and softkill (green) launchers

NOTE: Mountains and neighboring vehicles reflect radio waves, thus creating radar clutter, which adversely affects radar-detection and radar-lock performance. The trajectories of top attack ATGMs like the FGM-148 Javelin (US) and Trigat (Germany) plunge down onto their targets. Not all active protection systems are designed to fire at the extreme elevations necessary to protect against such munitions. RPGs fired at a steep downward angle from elevated positions can pose a similar threat. Only the *softkill components* of Afghanit are capable of dealing with top-attack missiles.

T-90M Proryv-3 Main Battle Tank (2019)

The T-90M Proryv-3 (Breakthrough-3) tank is an improved version of the T-90 and was first publicly revealed in 2017. The first of these modernized T-90M tanks was delivered to Russian troops in April 2020. The main features include the replacement of the Kontakt-5 Explosive Reactive Armor (ERA) on previous models with the **Relikt ERA** which provides superior protection against tandem warheads and reduces the penetration of Armor-Piercing Fin-Stabilizing Discarding Sabot rounds. The T-90M is equipped with a new turret module, a powerful 125 mm gun and **"Kalina"** fire control system with an integrated targeting suite, as well as a remote-controlled anti-aircraft gun **"UDP T05BV-1"**. The **2A46M-5, 125 mm smoothbore gun** fires several types of ammunition, including high-explosive anti-tank (HEAT-FS), and high explosive fragmentation (HE-FRAG), and armor-piercing fin-stabilized discarding sabot (APFSDS) rounds—as well as guided anti-tank missiles that can destroy tanks up to five kilometers away. In 2016, the Krasnogorsk plant finished testing the Irbis-K night-vision sighting system for the T-80U and T-90, with first deliveries in 2017. The Irbis-K mercury-cadmium-telluride (MCT) matrix thermal sight is capable of identifying targets at ranges up to 3,240 meters during both day and night. The T-90M is also fitted with an additional optoelectronic system for over-the-horizon targets. The target acquisition system tracks selected targets automatically. It is claimed that the new tank is 15-20% more accurate than its predecessor. The original T-90's 840 hp V-84MS engine was replaced with the 1,130 hp V-92S2F engine with a more favorable power/weight ratio. There are almost 500 T-90 and T-90A's in Russia's inventory and as many as 400 of these can be upgraded to T-90M.

1. 2A46M-5 Main Gun
2. Relikt ERA
3. Commander's RWS
4. Commander's Panoramic Sight
5. SOSNA-U sight
6. Gunner's Secondary Sight

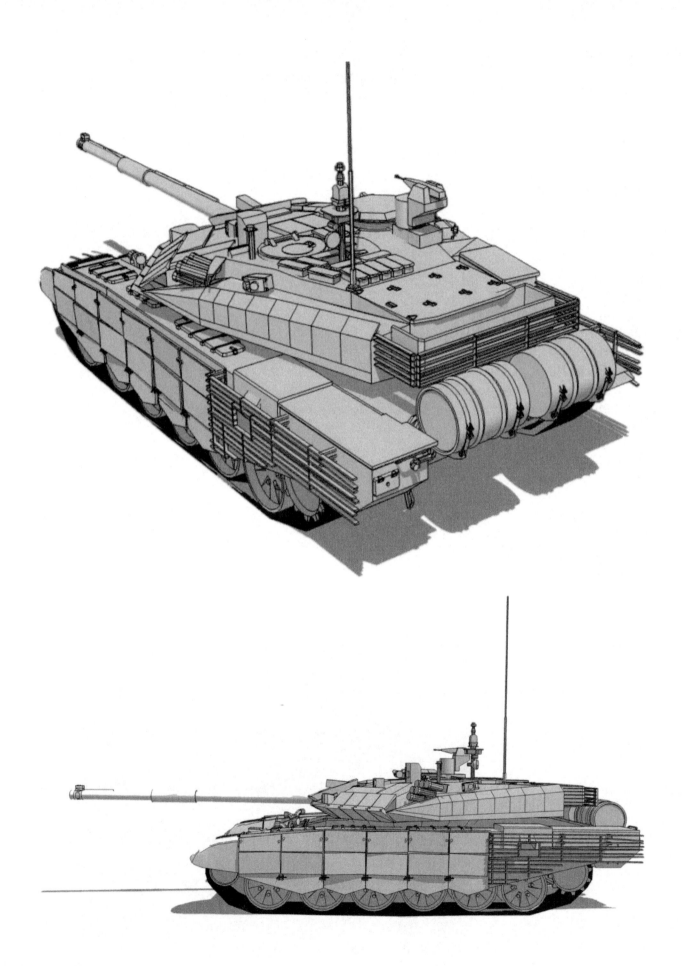

T-90M Specifications

Entered service	2019
Crew	3 men
Dimensions and weight	
Weight	46.5 t
Length (gun fwd)	9.53 m
Hull length	6.86 m
Width	3.78 m
Height	2.23 m
Armament	
Main gun	2A46M-5 125 mm smoothbore
ATGW	9M119 Refleks
Machine guns	1 x 12.7 mm, 1 x 7.62 mm
Elevation range	- 6 to + 14 degrees
Traverse range	360 degrees
Ammunition load	
Main gun	43 rounds
Machine guns	300 x 12.7 mm, 1 250 x 7.62 mm rounds
Mobility	
Engine	V-92S2 diesel
Engine power	1,000 hp
Max. road speed	60 km/h
Range	550 km
Maneuverability	
Gradient	60%
Side slope	40%
Vertical step	0.8 m
Trench	2.85 m
Fording	1.2 m
Fording with snorkle	5 m (with 20-minute preparation)

Russian inflatable decoy tank. Incredibly detailed compared to others

T-90M

Improvements include a new advanced fire control system "Kalina" (with integrated combat information and control systems), improved armor on the ammo carousel, a new upgraded gun 2A46M-5, a new 1130 hp V-92S2F engine, an enhanced environmental control system, and satellite navigation systems.

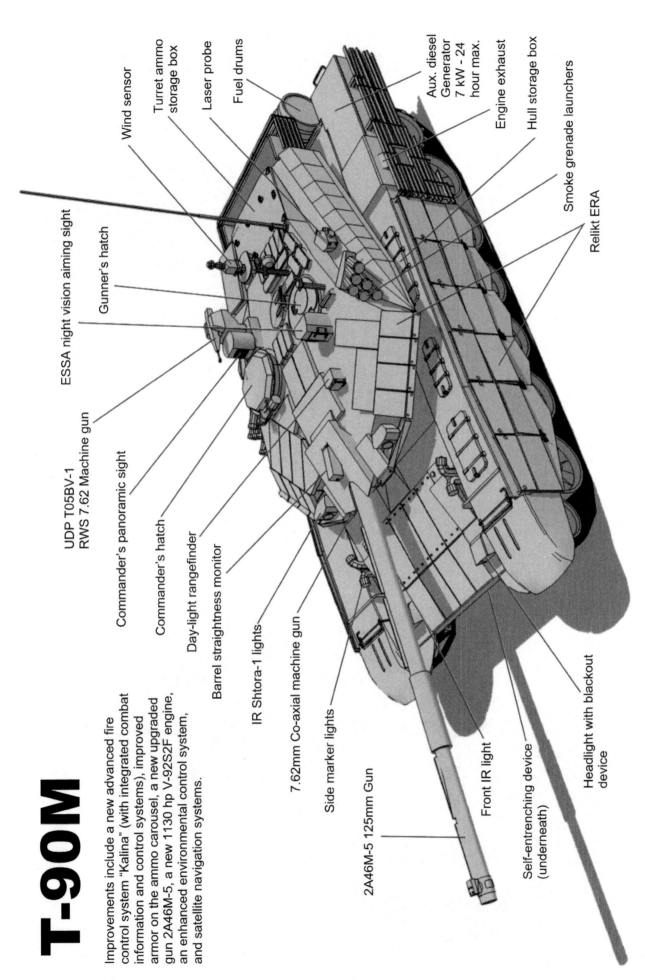

Wind sensor

Turret ammo storage box

Laser probe

Fuel drums

Aux. diesel Generator 7 kW - 24 hour max.

Engine exhaust

Hull storage box

Smoke grenade launchers

Relikt ERA

ESSA night vision aiming sight

Gunner's hatch

UDP T05BV-1 RWS 7.62 Machine gun

Commander's panoramic sight

Commander's hatch

Day-light rangefinder

Barrel straightness monitor

IR Shtora-1 lights

7.62mm Co-axial machine gun

Side marker lights

2A46M-5 125mm Gun

Front IR light

Self-entrenching device (underneath)

Headlight with blackout device

T-90MS Tagil Main Battle Tank (2017)

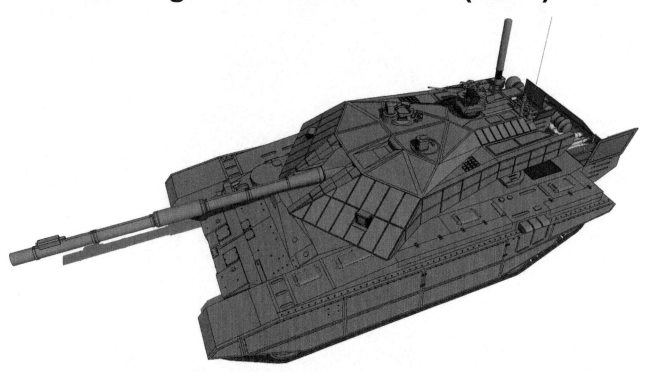

Although primarily developed for export, the T-90MS has been offered to the Russian army. Some of the T-90MS ammunition is stowed in a removable turret bustle at the rear to avoid the risks of explosion and improve crew survivability.

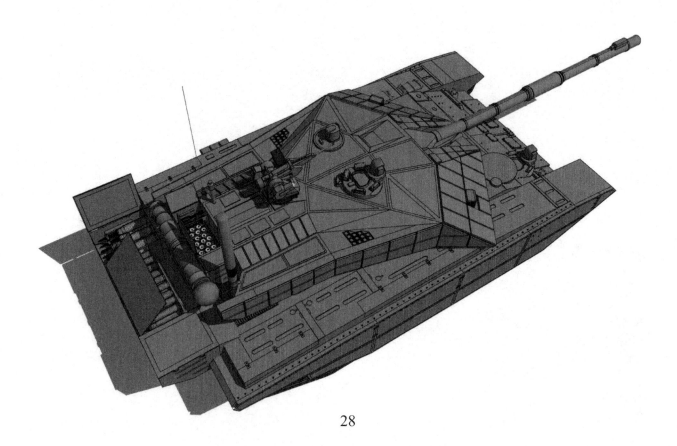

T-14 Armata Main Battle Tank (2022)

The T-14 program has experienced schedule delays, cost overruns, and overeager production estimates. Russia prioritized the T-90M over the more ambitious Armata tank, a highly-sophisticated, but less reliable vehicle. T-14 has a crew of three seated in an armored capsule at the front of the Hull. The driver is on the left, gunner in the middle and commander on the right. Entry and exit are through three top hatches. It has one 2A82-1M 125 mm main gun with autoloader in the unmanned turret that is digitally controlled, a 30 mm cannon, and a 12.7 mm machine gun. The gun is capable of firing guided missiles like the ***9M119M1 Invar-M*** which has an effective range of 100 m to 5 km, and can engage low-flying air targets such as helicopters, with a new ***3UBK21 Sprinter ATGM*** with an effective range up to 12 km developed specifically for it. The T-14 was designed to sustain direct hit by any current anti-tank munitions as well as robust heat signature reduction measures. The T-14 has a Ka band ***AESA radar*** as part of its detection system and a more powerful diesel engine mounted in the rear.

1. 9M119M1 Invar-M ATGM - It is able to penetrate 37 in. (900 mm) steel armor and has an effective range of 5 km.
2. Telnik HE-frag controlled detonation shell.

3. Vacuum I 0.9 to 1 m long penetrator sabot round specifically developed for the 2A82-1M.

Kord 12.7 mm Machine Gun
Installed above turret roof mounted commander's sight, it is designed to attack lightly-armored ground targets up to 2 km. It is capable of destroying incoming projectiles at a max speed of 3,000 meters per second. The gun is around 500 mm in length. It has a rate of fire of 600 to 700 rounds per minute. The muzzle velocity is estimated at 860 m/sec. The gun has 300 rounds fed from right side.

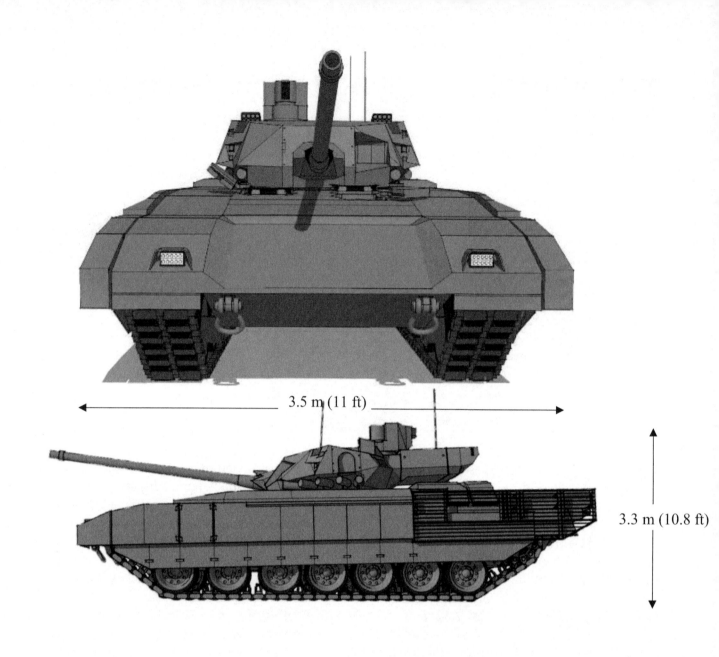

3.5 m (11 ft)

3.3 m (10.8 ft)

8.7 m (29 ft)

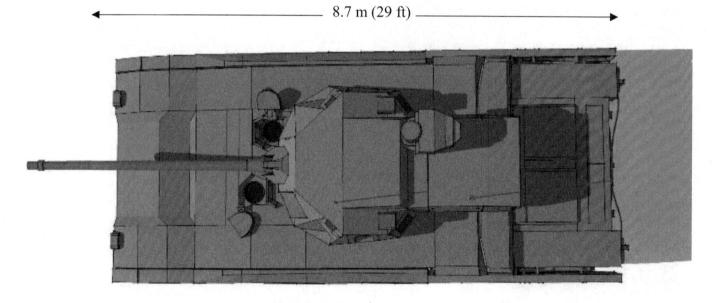

Protection

NII Stali Upper Hemispherical Protection Complex's two steerable cartridges with 12 charges and a turret top vertical launch system with two similar charges.

The T-14 has active and passive protection systems. The active protection systems fires a counter-projectile to hit the incoming projectile midair, before it hits the tank. The passive protection system has the capability to bear the high kinetic energy of the incoming round and sacrifice itself to protect the crew inside. The Armata has a reduced radar signature and special paint that reduces the tank's IR signature. The **NII Stali Upper Hemispherical Protection Complex** consists of two steerable cartridges with 12 charges and a turret top vertical launch system with two similar charges. These launch salvos of projectiles instantly creating a thick, multi-spectral smoke screens designed to defeat guided missiles, laser and targeting systems by blocking infrared, visible light to protect the tank from Hellfire, TOW and BILL, or Brimstone, JAGM, Javelin or Spike missiles, as well as from nearly vertical top-attack by sensor-fused weapons (SFW).

The **Afghanit active protection system** consists of five hard-kill cartridges/ canisters on each side at the bottom portion of the turret. They cover 60 degrees on each side of the turret. When a threat incoming from rear side is detected, the turret turns to intercept that threat projectile. A cartridge fires an electronically-activated charge towards the incoming projectile to damage or destroy it. APS has sensors mounted on each side of the turret, covering the rear and front quadrants left and right. The sensor is said to have the capability to detect, and simultaneously track and locate 40 land targets and 25 air targets.

In case of the T-14 and T-15 Armata vehicles, Afghanit utilizes ten launcher tubes covering only the frontal ~120° arc. On the Kurganets-25 and on the latest prototypes of the Bumerang, the Afghanit APS uses smaller tubes; depending on prototype five or six for each side (so 10 to 12 per vehicle), covering approximately a 200° arc at the left and right side of the vehicle, leaving the rear and front exposed.

31

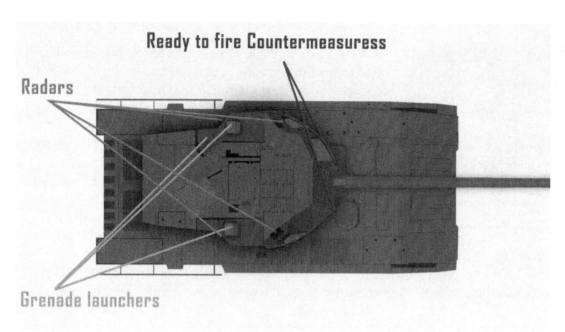

Afghanit radars and launcher locations

Armor protection

The hull is made up of a modular armor system made of steel, ceramics and composite materials. Armata is protected by Malachit Dual Explosive Reactive Armor on the hull and turret on the front, side and top. The tank is anticipated to offer up to STANAG 4569 Level 5 protection. The armor offers protection levels of 1000–1100 mm vs APFSDS and 1200–1400 mm vs HEAT. The

external fuel tanks (12) positioned on the engine's sides also add protection. Unlike the jettisonable barrels used on previous Russian tanks, these external tanks are fixed, and, therefore, are likely to be consumed first to reduce vulnerability in combat. T-14's floor is reinforced with an additional armor plate for counter-mine and counter IED protection, and it has a jamming system to detonate radio-controlled anti-tank mines. The steel plate (44C-SV-W) is lighter to reduce vehicle weight.

Bar Armor / Slat Armor / Cage Armor

The rear of the tank is fitted with bar armor to provide added protection against anti-tank rocket-propelled grenades (RPGs). Bar armor is designed to disrupt the shaped charge of the warhead by either crushing it, preventing optimal detonation from occurring, or by damaging the fuzing mechanism.

Situational Awareness

the T-14 panoramic sight XM1209 is integrated with the tank's radar and robotic mechanisms quickly rotates the panoramic sight.

Six (6) omnidirectional High-Definition cameras are connected to the Afghanit active protection system allowing it to:
• Work with the radar
• Avoid false positives
• Work under conditions of electronic warfare
• Detect laser irradiation on the tank
The crew would have poor situation awareness if the camera setup and video feeds were to fail.

The commander and gunner have largely identical *multispectral image sights*, with visible electromagnetic spectrum and thermography channels and *laser rangefinders*. The detection distance of tank-sized objects for both sights is 7,500 m (8,000) in daylight, through the TV/periscopic channel, and ≈3,500 m at night through the thermal channel. There is also a backup night-vision capable sight, with 2,000/1,000 m respective detection distances.

Radar

The T-14 pulse-Doppler radar is able to calculate the trajectory of projectiles like artillery and automatically calculate the coordinates of the positions of the enemy to provide automatic return fire.

Night-vision

The *Irbis-K night-vision sighting system* is capable of identifying targets at ranges up to 3,240 meters during both day and night.

Communications

The T-14 uses highly protected communication channels that connect a group of T-14s and the command post.

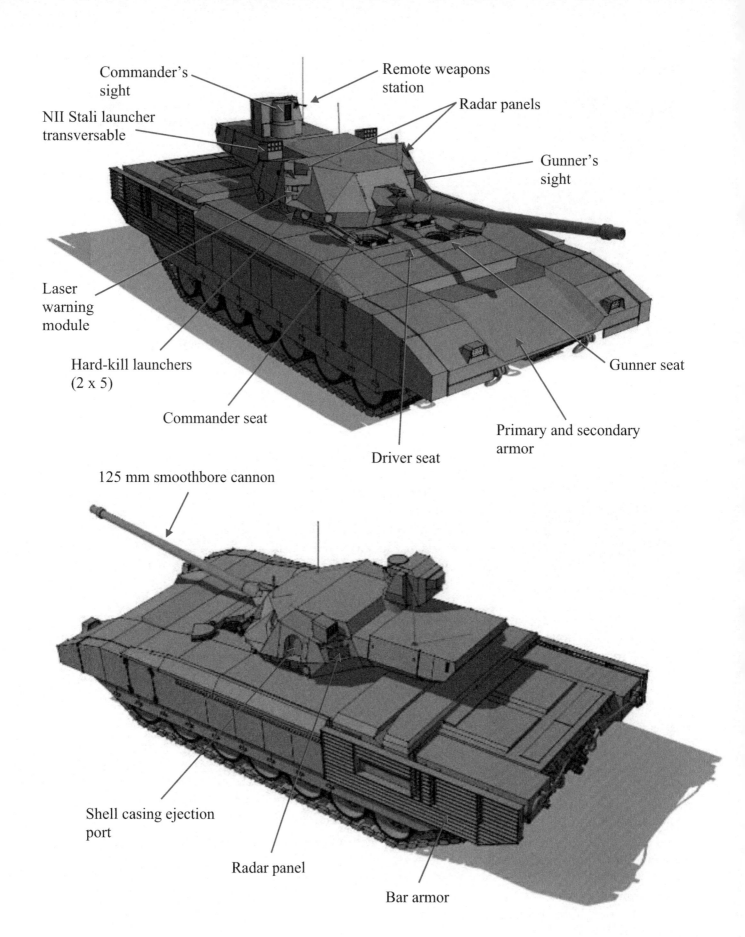

Commander's sight

Remote weapons station

Radar panels

NII Stali launcher transversable

Gunner's sight

Laser warning module

Hard-kill launchers (2 x 5)

Commander seat

Driver seat

Gunner seat

Primary and secondary armor

125 mm smoothbore cannon

Shell casing ejection port

Radar panel

Bar armor

T-14 ARMATA SPECIFICATIONS

Weight (tons)	55	**Speed (kph/mph)**	80/50
Length	8.7 m (29 ft)	**Operational Range (km/mi)**	510 / 310
Width	3.5 m (11 ft)	**Power/weight**	31hp/t
Height	3.3 m (10.8 ft)		
Crew	4		

Weapons:

Primary

2A82-1M 125 mm (4.92 in) smoothbore cannon with 45 rounds (32 in the autoloader), fire rate of 10–12 rpm (rounds per minute) at an effective range of up to 7 kilometers, left side casing ejection port. Can fire a wide range of ammunition: including armor-piercing fin-stabilized discarding sabot (APFSDS) projectiles, guided missiles, high-explosive anti-tank (HEAT-FS) shells, air-burst HE-Frag shells and other types of rounds. The Vacuum-1 APFSDS round, developed for the 2A82-1M gun, has a penetrator that is 900 mm long, and is said to be capable of penetrating 1 m of RHA equivalent at a distance of 2 km. The new controlled-detonation Telnik HE-Frag shell is available and has entered service. The gun is capable of firing guided missiles like the 9M119M1 Invar-M which has an effective range of 100 m to 5 km, and can engage low-flying air targets such as helicopters, with a new 3UBK21 Sprinter ATGM with a maximum effective range up to 12 km. 70% increase in accuracy while moving compared to the older 125 mm Soviet cannons. Future version may use the smoothbore 2A83 152 mm tank gun.

Secondary

12.7 × 108mm Kord (GRAU index 6P49) machine gun with 300 rounds a 7.62×54mmR Pecheneg PKP (GRAU Index: 6P41) or a PKTM (6P7K) co-axial machine gun with 1,000 rounds. All guns are remotely controlled.

Turret may also be fitted with a Shipunov 2A42 30 mm cannon for use against various targets, including low-flying aircraft and helicopters.

Armor

44S-sv-Sh Glacis: 900 mm vs APFSDS and 1400 mm vs HEAT. Internal armored capsule with more than 900 mm RHA equivalent. Malachit (4th generation Explosive Reactive Armor) can reduce penetration of APFSDS rounds.

Defensive Systems

Afghanit active protection system (APS), includes a millimeter-wave radar to detect, track, and intercept incoming anti-tank munitions, both kinetic energy penetrators and tandem-charges. It is not built to shoot upwards to defend against top-attack munitions.

NII Stali Upper Hemisphere Protection Complex, consists of two steerable cartridges with 12 smaller charges each, and a turret-top VLS with two more similar cartridges corresponding to the soft kill APS.

Sensors

Up to 40 airborne or 25 ground targets down to 0.3 m (12 in) in size can be tracked simultaneously by the 26.5–40 GHz active electronically scanned array radar.

The commander and gunner have multispectral image sights, with visible electromagnetic spectrum and thermography channels and laser rangefinder. Commander has a 360° field of view. The detection distance of tank-sized objects for both sights is 7,500 m by day, 3,500 m by night.

Night-vision capable sight has 2,000/1,000 m detection distances.

In addition to periscopes, the driver has a forward-looking infrared camera and a number of zooming closed-circuit video cameras installed for 360-degree all-round vision.

Communications   Highly protected communication channels connect a group of T-14s and the command post.

Engine   ChTZ 12H360 (A-85-3A) diesel engine 1,500 hp, moderated to 1,200 hp in normal operation

Transmission   12-speed automatic transmission (16-gears, including reverse - estimate)

Notes   An unmanned version of the T-14 is in development.

T-14 in arctic camo

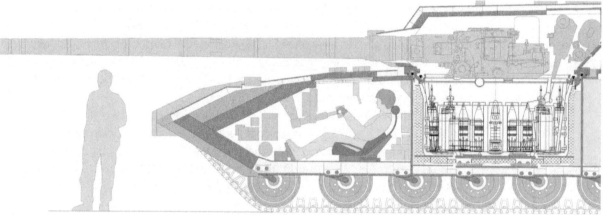

T-14 Cross-section showing crew module and autoloader

2C2S Sprut-SD Airborne Light Tank (2005)

The 2S25 Sprut-SD has firepower comparable with modern main battle tanks and outperforms light tanks and tank destroyers. It is armed with a fully-stabilized 125 mm smoothbore gun, fitted with an autoloader. This gun is also used to launch anti-tank guided missiles in the same manner as ordinary projectiles. Laser-guided anti-tank missiles have a range of effective fire of up to 5 km. Missiles can also be used against low-flying helicopters. A total of 40 rounds including missiles are carried for the main gun. An autoloader holds 22 of them. The 2S25 Sprut SD has a rate of fire of 7 rounds per minute. Vehicle is fitted with a modern fire control system. Protection of the Sprut-SD is extremely limited. Its front arc only provides protection against 12.7 mm rounds. All-round protection is against small-arms fire and artillery shell splinters only. Protection can be increased with add-on armor and countermeasures system. It is fitted with NBC protection and automatic fire extinguishing systems. Currently only a relatively small number of the original Sprut-SD light tanks are in service with the Russian airborne units.

SPECIFICATIONS

	2C2S Sprut-SD	Sprut-SDM1
Entered service	2005	2016
Crew	3	3
Weight	18 t	18 t
Length (gun forward)	7.2 m	7.08 m
Hull length	~ 6.5 m	~ 5.8 m
Width	3.2 m	3.15 m
Height	~ 2.2 m	3.05 m
Main gun	125 mm smoothbore	125 mm smoothbore
	40 rounds	40 rounds
ATGW	?	?
Machine guns	1 x 7.62 mm	2 x 7.62 mm
	2,000 rounds	2,000 rounds
Elevation range	- 5 to + 15 degrees	
Traverse range	360 degrees	
Engine	2V-06-2S diesel (510 hp)	UTD-29 diesel (450 hp)
Max. speed	road speed 70 km/h	road speed 70 km/h
	speed on water 10 km/h	speed on water 7 km/h
Range	500 km	500 km
Gradient	60%	60%
Side slope	30%	30%
Vertical step	~ 0.9 m	~ 0.8 m
Trench	~ 1.8 m	~ 2.8 m
Fording	Amphibious	Amphibious

Sprut-SDM1 Light Amphibious Tank (2016)

The Sprut-SDM1 is a modernized version of the previous Sprut-SD. It has the chassis of the new BMD-4M airborne combat vehicle and uses some fire control elements of the T-90MS main battle tank. The Sprut-SDM1 was delivered for official military trials in 2020. These trials should be completed in 2021-2022. It is armed with a fully-stabilized 2A75M 125 mm smoothbore gun. It can fire all standard 125 mm ammunition used by T-72 and T-90 series tanks. Maximum range of fire is 2-2.5 km. There is an automatic ammunition loading system.

The Sprut-SDM1 can launch anti-tank guided missiles. The laser-guided anti-tank missiles are derived from 9M119M1 (Invar-M) missile. These have a range of up to 5 km and can also target low-flying helicopters. A total of 40 rounds including missiles are carried for the main gun. The autoloader holds 22 of them. Remaining 18 rounds are stored inside the hull. Typical ammunition load consists of 20 HE-FRAG rounds, 14 APFSDS anti-tank rounds and 6 anti-tank guided missiles. This tank has a rate of fire of 7 rounds per minute. Spent cases are automatically ejected behind the turret.

There is a coaxial 7.62 mm machine gun. The Sprut-SDM1 is fitted with additional remotely controlled weapon station, armed with a 7.62 mm machine gun. On water it is propelled by two waterjets. Vehicle is sea worthy up to Sea State 3. Even when afloat, it can fire its main gun in limited traverse range. The Sprut-SDM1 can embark and disembark from amphibious assault ships on its own.

2S42 Lotus Self-propelled Mortar (2020)

The Lotus can engage armored vehicles with direct or indirect fire. It is armed with a 120 mm breech-loaded mortar (manually loaded) with an armor-piercing round that can penetrate a 600-650 mm steel plate at a range of 1,000 m and the range of fire from 1 to 13 km, using rifled rounds. It is also compatible with Kitolov-2M laser-guided rounds. These have a maximum range of 10 km and a hit probability of 80 to 90%. Maximum rate of fire is claimed to be 6-8 rounds per minute. It is claimed that a total of 40 rounds of ammunition are carried for the main gun.

The 2S42 Lotus is fitted with a 7.62 mm remotely controlled weapon station and smoke grenade dischargers. It uses a modified chassis of a 2S25 Sprut-SD or the newer Sprut-SDM-1 airborne light tank. Engine compartment is located at the rear. The 2S42 Lotus has a hydropneumatic suspension with adjustable ground clearance. Maximum road speed is up to 70 km/h. Maximum off-road speed is up to 30-40 km/h. The 2S42 Lotos is fully amphibious. On water it is propelled by 2 waterjets. Vehicle is sea worthy up to a Sea State 3.

40

2S42 Lotus SPECIFICATIONS

Crew	4
Weight	18 tons
Length (gun forward)	~ 7 m
Hull length	~ 5.8 m
Width	~ 3.15 m
Height	~ 3.05 m
Armament	
Main gun	120 mm howitzer/mortar
Barrel length	?
Machine guns	1 x 7.62 mm
Projectile weight	17.3 kg
Max firing range	13 km
Max rate of fire	6 - 8 rpm
Elevation range	- 4 to + 80 degrees
Traverse range	360 degrees
Ammunition load	
Main gun	40 rounds
Machine guns	~ 1,500 rounds
Mobility	
Engine	2V-06-2 diesel
Engine power	450 hp
Max. speed	
Road	70 km/h
Off-road	30-40 km/h
On water	7 km/h
Range	500 km
Maneuverability	
Gradient	60%
Side slope	30%
Vertical step	~ 0.9 m
Trench	~ 1.8 m
Fording	Amphibious

Inflatable decoy radar.

Other inflatable decoys.

Other books we publish on Amazon.com

Customer reviews
★★★★½ 4.6 out of 5

Customer reviews
★★★½☆ 3.6 out of 5

Customer reviews
★★★★☆ 4.2 out of 5

Customer reviews
★★★★★ 5 out of 5

T-54/T-55 Main Battle Tank (1947-present)

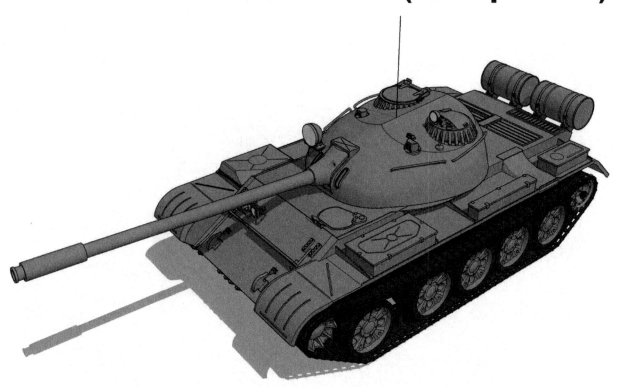

We decided to include the T-54/T-55 because the T-54/55 series is the most-produced tank in history. Estimated production numbers for the series range from 96,500 to 100,000. So, the likelihood exists that you may come up against one someday. The T-54A entered production in 1954 and service in 1955. It had night vision equipment for the driver and a 100 mm D-10T2S tank gun with STP-2 "Tsyklon" 2-plane stabilizer. It also was equipped with an L-2 "Luna" infrared searchlight, a TPN-1-22-11 IR gunner's sight, and an OU-3 IR commander's searchlight.

The T-55 included NBC system offering protection against the blast of a nuclear weapon and (radioactive) particulate filtration, but not against external gamma radiation or gas. It was fitted with the new V-55 12-cylinder four-stroke one-chamber, 38.88-litre water-cooled diesel engine developing 581 hp (433 kW). The gun could fire 4 rounds per minute and the BK5M HEAT rounds which penetrated 390 mm (15 in) thick armor.

← 9 m (29.5 ft) →

T-55 Specifications (T-55)

Mass	36 tons (39.7 ST)
Length	9.00 m (with gun forward)
Width	3.37 m
Height	2.40 m
Crew	4
Armor	205 mm turret front, 130 mm turret sides, 60 mm turret rear, 30 mm turret roof, 120 mm hull front at 60° (100 mm after 1949), 79 mm hull upper sides, 20 mm hull lower sides, 60 mm at 0° hull rear, 20 mm hull bottom, 33-16 mm hull roof
Main armament	D-10T 100 mm rifled gun (43 rounds)
Secondary armament	7.62 mm SGMT coaxial machine gun, (12.7 mm DShK heavy machine gun)
Engine Model	V-55(V-54) V-12 water-cooled. 38.88-l diesel, 500 hp (373 kW) up to 800 hp (597 kW)
Power/weight	14.6 hp (10.4 kW) / ton
Transmission	Mechanical (synchromesh), 5 forward, 1 reverse gears
Suspension	Torsion bar
Gnd clearance	0.425 m
Fuel capacity	580 L internal, 320 L external (less on early T54), 400 L jettisonable rear fuel drums
Max. speed	51 km/h (31.6 mph)

T-55A Main Battle Tank (1961)

In its long service life, the T-55 has been upgraded many times. Early T-55s were fitted with a new TSh-2B-32P sight. In 1959, some tanks received mountings for the PT-55 mine clearing system or the BTU/BTU-55 plough. In 1967, the improved 3BM-8 APDS round, which could penetrate 275 mm thick armor at a range of 2 km, was introduced. In 1970, new and old T-55 tanks had the loader's hatch modified to mount the 12.7 mm DShK machine gun, to deal with the threat of attack helicopters. Starting in 1974, T-55 tanks received the KTD-1 or KTD-2 laser rangefinder in an armored box over the mantlet of the main gun, as well as the R-123 or R-123M radio set. Simultaneously, efforts were made to modernize and increase the lifespan of the drive train.

A wide array of upgrades in different price ranges are provided by many manufacturers in different countries, intended to bring the T-54/55 up to the capabilities of newer MBTs, at a lower cost. Upgrades include new engines, explosive reactive armor, new main armament such as 120 mm or 125 mm guns, active protection systems, and fire control systems with range-finders or thermal sights. These improvements make it a potent main battle tank (MBT) for the low-end budget, even to this day. 27,500 T-55, T-55A, T-55K1, T-55K2, T-55K3, T-55AK1, T-55AK2 and T-55AK3 tanks were produced between 1955 and 1981.

T-62 Main Battle Tank (1961)

At least 2,000 T-62 tanks were inherited from the Soviet Union. About 761 were in active service in 1995; 191 were in active service and 1,929 in storage as of January 2000. During 2013 all the T-62 tanks were (allegedly) scrapped, except that Russia keeps supplying T-62s to Syria as recently as 2018 (T-62M and T-62MV). The T-62 was the first production tank armed with a smoothbore tank gun that could fire APFSDS rounds at higher velocities.

T-62MV, fitted with Kontakt-1 ERA on turret front and hull front and sides

T-61 Specifications

Mass	37 t (41 short tons; 36 long tons)
Length	9.34 m (30 ft 8 in) with barrel in forward position
	6.63 m (21 ft 9 in) hull only
Width	3.30 m (10 ft 10 in)
Height	2.40 m (7 ft 10 in)
Crew	4 (commander, driver, gunner, loader)

Armor Cast turret 214 (242 after 1972) mm turret front, 153 mm turret sides, 97 mm turret rear, 40 mm turret roof, Hull 102 mm at 60° hull front, 79 mm hull upper sides, 15 mm hull lower sides, 46 mm at 0° hull rear, 20 mm hull bottom, 31 mm hull roof

Main armament	115 mm U-5TS (2A20) smoothbore gun
Secondary	7.62 mm PKT coaxial general-purpose machine gun (2500 rounds)
Armament	12.7 mm DShK 1938/46 antiaircraft heavy machine gun
Engine	V-55 12-cylinder 4-stroke one-chamber 38.88-liter water-cooled diesel, 581 hp (433 kW)
Power/weight	14.5 hp/ton (10.8 kW/ton)
Suspension	torsion bar
Gnd clearance	425 mm (16.7 in)
Fuel capacity	960 L, 1360 L with two 200-liter extra fuel tanks
Operational	450 km (280 mi) on road (650 km (400 mi) with two 200 l (53 US gal; 44 imp gal) extra
Range	fuel tanks), 320 km (200 mi) cross-country (450 km (280 mi) with two extra fuel tanks)
Max. speed	50 km/h (31 mph) (road), 40 km/h (25 mph) (cross country)

Russian Tank Ammunition

APFSDS-T - Armor-piercing fin-stabilized discarding sabot

3VBM22/3BM59 (3BM59 "Svinets-1")
Entered service: 2002. Utilizes a new depleted uranium sabot.
Used on 2A46M-5 with new autoloader.
    Projectile dimension: 740 mm estimated 30:1 L/d
    Round weight: ? kg
    Projectile weight (including sabot): ?
    Penetrator weight: estimated 4.4 kg [620mm x 22mm penetrator]
    Muzzle velocity: 1,650 m/s?
    Muzzle energy: 12 MJ?
    Penetration: 540 mm at 0° at 2000 m, 315 mm at 60°

3VBM23/3BM60 (3BM60 "Svinets-2")
Entered service: 2002. Utilizes a new sabot design. Uses a Tungsten Alloy penetrator of
increased length compared to previous generation Russian APFSDS ammunition. Used on
2A46M-5 with new autoloader.
    Projectile dimension: 735mm x 21mm L/D: 35:1
    Round weight: 22.0 kg
    Projectile weight (including sabot): 8.4 kg
    Penetrator weight: 4.1 kg (Estimated) [620mm x 22mm Penetrator]
    Muzzle velocity: 1,660 m/s
    Muzzle energy: 6.06 MJ
    Penetration: 515 mm at 0° at 2000 m, 300 mm at 60° at 2,000 m

3VBM?/3BM69 "Vacuum-1"
Entered service: 2005. Utilizes a new sabot. Reported to be uranium alloy. For 2A82/2A82-1M
cannon on T-80UM-2/T-14s.
    Country of origin: Russia
    Projectile dimension: 900 mm
    Round weight: ?
    Projectile weight (including sabot): ?
    Projectile weight: estimated 11 kg
    Muzzle velocity: 2050 m/s
    Muzzle energy: 15–24 MJ (described 15MJ probably refer to high-explosive shell)
    Penetration: 1,000 mm at 0°

3VBM?/3BM70 "Vacuum-2"
Entered service: 2005. Utilizes a new sabot. Reported to be tungsten alloy.
    Projectile dimension: ?
    Round weight: ?
    Projectile weight (including sabot): ?
    Muzzle velocity: ?
    Muzzle energy: ?
    Penetration: 1,200 mm?? at 0° at 2,000 m

HEAT-FS - High-explosive anti-tank fin stabilized.

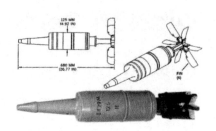

3VBM22/3BM59 (3BM59 "Svinet-1")
Entered service: 2002. Utilizes a new depleted uranium sabot.
Used on 2A46M-5 with new autoloader.
    Projectile dimension: 740 mm estimated 30:1 L/d
    Round weight: ? kg
    Projectile weight (including sabot): ?
    Penetrator weight: estimated 4.4 kg [620mm x 22mm penetrator]
    Muzzle velocity: 1,650 m/s?
    Muzzle energy: 12 MJ?
    Penetration: 540 mm at 0° at 2,000 m, 315 mm at 60°

3VBM23/3BM60 (3BM60 "Svinets-2")
Entered service: 2002. Utilizes a new sabot design. Uses a Tungsten Alloy penetrator of
increased length compared to previous generation Russian APFSDS ammunition. Used on
2A46M-5 with new autoloader.
    Projectile dimension: 735mm x 21mm L/D: 35:1
    Round weight: 22.0 kg
    Projectile weight (including sabot): 8.4 kg
    Penetrator weight: 4.1 kg (Estimated) [620mm x 22mm Penetrator]
    Muzzle velocity: 1,660 m/s
    Muzzle energy: 6.06 MJ
    Penetration: 515 mm at 0° at 2,000 m, 300 mm at 60° at 2,000 m

3VBM?/3BM69 "Vacuum-1"
Entered service: 2005. Utilizes a new sabot. Reported to be uranium alloy.
For 2A82/2A82-1M cannon on T-80UM-2/T-14s.
    Projectile dimension: 900 mm
    Round weight: ?
    Projectile weight (including sabot): ?
    Projectile weight: estimated 11 kg
    Muzzle velocity: 2,050 m/s
    Muzzle energy: 15–24 MJ (described 15MJ probably refer to high-explosive shell)
    Penetration: 1,000 mm at 0°

3VBM?/3BM70 "Vacuum-2"
Entered service: 2005. Utilizes a new sabot. Reported to be tungsten alloy.
    Projectile dimension: ?
    Round weight: ?
    Projectile weight (including sabot): ?
    Muzzle velocity: ?
    Muzzle energy: ?
    Penetration: 1,200 mm?? at 0° at 2000 m

HE-frag-FS - High explosive fragmentation fin stabilized. General purpose round.

3VOF22/3OF19

Entered service in 1962. Uses the 3V-21 detonator (mass = 0.431 kg, reliability = 0.98). The 90% lethal zone for infantry is reported to be 40 m wide and 20 m deep.
Round weight: 33.0 kg
Projectile weight: 23.0 kg
Muzzle velocity: 850 m/s
Max dispersion: 0.23 mil (0.23 mrad)
Charge weight: 3.148 kg
Charge: TNT

3VOF36/3OF26

Entered service in 1970. Uses the 3V-21 detonator (mass = 0.431 kg, reliability = 0.98). The projectile creates between 600 and 2,000 fragments. The body is made up of 45Kh1 steel or 60S2 high-fragmentation steel for modern projectiles. Modern projectiles creates up to 2,500 effective fragments.
Round weight: 33.0 kg
Projectile weight: 23.0 kg
Muzzle velocity: 850 m/s
Max dispersion: 0.23 mil (0.23 mrad)
Charge weight: 3.4 kg
Charge: A-IX-2 (73% RDX, 23% aluminum powder, phlegmatized with 4% wax) 3.4 kg

3VOF128/3OF82

Entered service: 2014. Uses the 3VM-18 programmable detonator. The projectile contains 450 tungsten rods, each weighing 3 grams and creates 2,500 fragments in a cone formation ahead of the projectile when air burst mode is set. Air burst mode for use against infantry, light vehicles and helicopters, delayed mode use against bunkers and other constructions. Is currently used on the 2A46M-5 gun, mounted on the T-90M.
Round weight: 33.0 kg
Projectile weight: 23.0 kg
Muzzle velocity: 850 m/s
Max dispersion: 0.23 mil (0.23 mrad)
Charge weight: 3.0 kg
Charge: A-IX-2 (73% RDX, 23% aluminum powder, phlegmatized with 4% wax) 3.0 kg

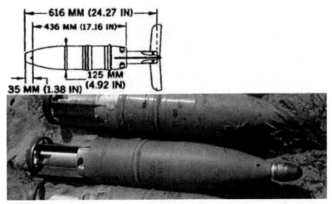

3OF26 HE-frag round

ATGW/ATGM

9M112 "Kobra"

The 9K112 Kobra (NATO reporting name is AT-8 Songster) is also fired from the 125 mm main guns of the T-64 and T-80 series of tanks
   Projectile weight: 23.2 kg
   Warhead weight: 4.5 kg
   Guidance system: Radio-command guided
   Range: 100 – 4000 m
   Penetration: Estimated at 700 mm (28 in) after ERA tandem charge HEAT

9M119 "Refleks"

The 9M119 Svir and 9M119M Refleks (NATO reporting name: AT-11 Sniper) anti-tank guided missile has semi-automatic laser beam-riding guidance and a tandem hollow-charge HEAT warhead. It has an effective range of 75 m to 5,000 m, and takes 17.6 seconds to reach maximum range. Refleks can penetrate about 900 mm (35 in) of steel armor and can also engage low-flying air targets such as helicopters.
   Projectile weight: 16.5 kg
   Warhead weight: 4.5 kg
   Guidance system: Laser-beam riding
   Range: 75 – 5000 m
   Penetration: Estimated at 900 mm (35 in) after ERA tandem charge HEAT

3UBK21 "Sprinter"

Designed for the 2A82-1M gun on T-14 Armata tanks, the 3UBK21 Sprinter has millimeter wave SACLOS guidance and a tandem shaped-charge HEAT warhead. It has an effective range of 50 m to 12,000 m. and can penetrate 950 mm (37 in) of steel armor after explosive reactive armor. It can also engage low-flying air targets such as helicopters.
   Projectile weight: ?
   Warhead weight: ?
   Guidance system: millimeter wave
   Range: 50 – 1,2000 m
   Penetration: Estimated at 950 mm (37 in) after ERA tandem charge HEAT

9K112 Kobra round in flight configuration

9M119 Refleks ATGM

Guided Shell

Sokol-1

The Sokol-1 guided shell is fired from the 125 mm main gun, it borrowed design from the 152mm artillery shell 3OF75 Santimetr-M and both have very similar appearance, but with an added shaped charge cap into its design similar to the M712 Copperhead, intended to defeat heavily armored targets. It uses the technique that is referred to as the Russian concept of impulse corrections (RCIC), an impulse steering flight control system to correct the projectile's trajectory.

   Projectile weight: 23.0 kg
   Muzzle velocity: 850 m/s
   Guidance system: Semi-Active Laser/Passive target contour-based
   Range: 0.1 – 5.0 km (direct fire)
          12 km (indirect fire)
   Warhead: High-explosive/700 mm (28 in) penetration shaped charge

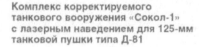

Комплекс корректируемого танкового вооружения «Сокол-1» с лазерным наведением для 125-мм танковой пушки типа Д-81

The Sokol-1 125-mm D-81 tank gun laser-guided artillery munition

Предназначен для поражения бронетанковой техники противника.

The munitions are used against armor.

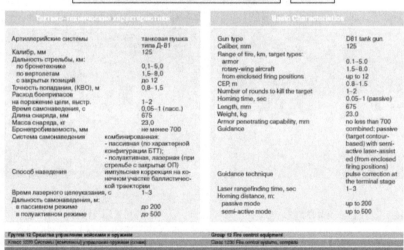

Тактико-технические характеристики		Basic Characteristics	
Артиллерийские системы	танковая пушка типа Д-81	Gun type	D81 tank gun
Калибр, мм	125	Caliber, mm	125
Дальность стрельбы, км:		Range of fire, km, target types:	
по бронетехнике	0,1–5,0	armor	0.1–5.0
по вертолетам	1,5–8,0	rotary-wing aircraft	1.5–8.0
с закрытых позиций	до 12	from enclosed firing positions	up to 12
Точность попадания, (КВО), м	0,8–1,5	CEP, m	0.8–1.5
Расход боеприпасов		Number of rounds to kill the target	1–2
на поражение цели, выстр.	1–2	Homing time, sec	0.05–1 (passive)
Время самонаведения, с	0,05–1 (пасс.)	Length, mm	675
Длина снаряда, мм	675	Weight, kg	23.0
Масса снаряда, кг	23,0	Armor penetrating capability, mm	no less than 700
Бронепробиваемость, мм	не менее 700	Guidance	combined: passive (target contour-based) with semi-active laser-assisted (from enclosed firing positions)
Система самонаведения	комбинированная: - пассивная (по характерной конфигурации БТТ); - полуактивная, лазерная (при стрельбе с закрытых ОП)		
Способ наведения	импульсная коррекция на конечном участке баллистической траектории	Guidance technique	pulse correction at the terminal stage
Время лазерного целеуказания, с	1–3	Laser rangefinding time, sec	1–3
Дальность самонаведения, м:		Homing distance, m:	
в пассивном режиме	до 200	passive mode	up to 200
в полуактивном режиме	до 500	semi-active mode	up to 500
Группа 12 Средства управления войсками и оружием		Group 12 Fire control equipment	
Класс 1230 Системы (комплексы) управления оружием (огнем)		Class 1230 Fire control systems, complex	

3UBK14F1/9M119F1

The 3UBK14F1 guided shell is fired from the 125 mm main gun, its design was modified from 9M119 missile, removing the rocket motor and replacing it with an extra Thermobaric warhead, turning it into a guided shell. Its range was decreased to 3.5 km, and it is claimed to be three times the explosive power of regular thermobaric variant 125 mm guided missiles.

   Projectile weight: 16.5 kg
   Muzzle velocity: 284 m/s
   Guidance system: Laser-beam riding
   Range: 0.1 – 3.5 km
   Warhead: Thermobaric estimated 15 kg TNT equivalent

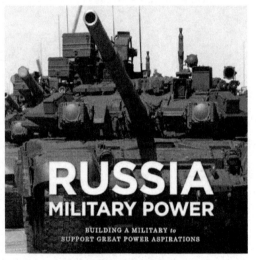

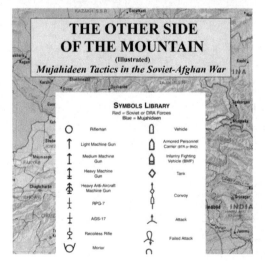

Russian Tank Tactics

Offense

A Russian tank in an offensive operates, as a rule, as part of a platoon, and can also be allocated for destruction of targets with direct fire during the preparation of the offensive. The tank is assigned the targets for the attack and the direction of the further offensive. The targets of a tank are usually enemy tanks, anti-tank guns, anti-tank missile emplacements and other fire weapons of the enemy located in the first trench and in the closest depth of his defense. The direction and distance to be covered is determined in such a way that the fulfillment of the immediate task of the company is ensured.[1] During the battle, the tank commander controls his crew by commands sent to the tank intercom or voice, and for target designation uses the system fire control. The infantry fighting vehicles and armored personnel carriers usually operate behind battle groups or on one of the flanks of the squad. There is little evidence of formal cross training within the tank crew.

The tank designated for direct fire, at the direction of the platoon commander secretly advances and takes a prepared firing position in advance or during fire preparation of the offensive. The crew prepares for the mission and conducts reconnaissance of targets. The tank commander prepares data for firing at the detected targets and makes up a *tank fire card*. With the beginning of the preparation of the offensive, the tank destroys or suppresses the designated and newly identified targets at the front line and in the nearest depth of enemy defenses. When going on the offensive after completing fire missions with direct fire, a tank with the approach of the remaining combat vehicles of the platoon, together with them, attacks the enemy and acts in accordance with the combat mission objectives and commands of the platoon commander.

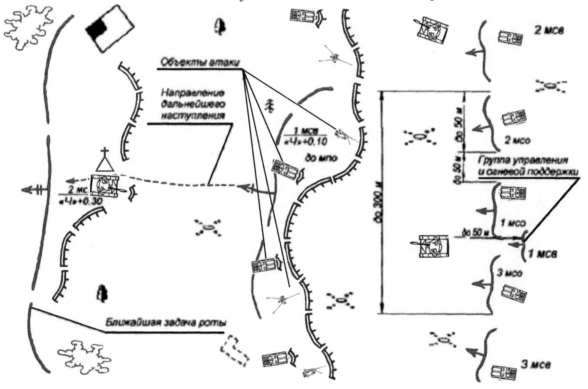

In all figures: Assume that radio communications exist between each vehicle depicted.

---

[1] Recent reports from Ukraine suggest an inability of the Russian Army to sustain a pursuit over 30 kilometers.

Defense

A tank in defense operates, as a rule, as part of a platoon, can be assigned to a fire ambush as well as stand out in the battalion armored group. He works in close interaction with a motorized rifle subunit, in the battle formations of which it goes to defend. The main and reserve firing positions are assigned to the tank, which are usually equipped behind the combat position of a motorized rifle subunit in such a way that cover fire for motorized riflemen and their safety when firing from a cannon is provided.

When developing a plan of attack, the tank commander must determine: which enemy, where and with what firing position to defeat when advancing, deploying, repelling an attack, destruction of the wedged enemy, including the procedure for supporting actions by fire motorized rifle unit; ensuring secrecy during preparation and execution of the assigned task. In the tasks for the crew members, the tank commander determines the order of their actions when occupying and changing firing positions, tasks for conducting reconnaissance and destroying targets to support the battle motorized rifle units, as well as the procedure for damage to a tank and other questions.

A fire ambush in defense is set up in order to inflict maximum damage by sudden direct fire, dagger fire, and the use of mines as explosive barriers. A tank platoon may be reinforced by sappers and flamethrowers. A fire ambush is usually organized in tank-hazardous areas in front of the forward edge, in depth of the company strongpoint (battalion defense area), in the intervals between them or on flanks, in places that make it difficult for the enemy to quickly deploy and conduct maneuvers for getting out of the line of fire.

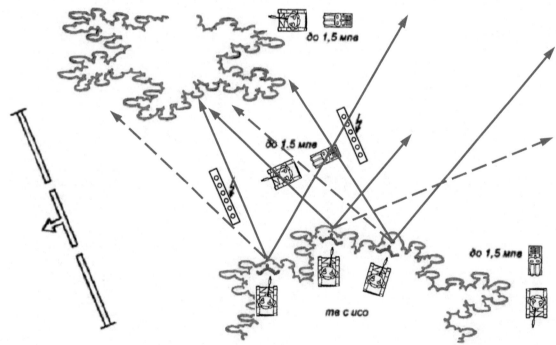

The position of the fire ambush should ensure the covert location of the tank and provide good conditions for observation, firing and escape routes. The most probable places for a Russian tank fire ambush position are reverse slopes of heights, folds of the terrain, outskirts of settlements, forest edges and dense shrubbery. Keep in mind that platoon leaders are normally lieutenants, but may sergeants. The authority of the platoon leader in company operations is limited. When attached to a motorized rifle battalion, especially in defensive operations, platoon leaders may be allowed more flexibility in the execution of their mission.

56

Diagram of a Strongpoint of a Tank Platoon

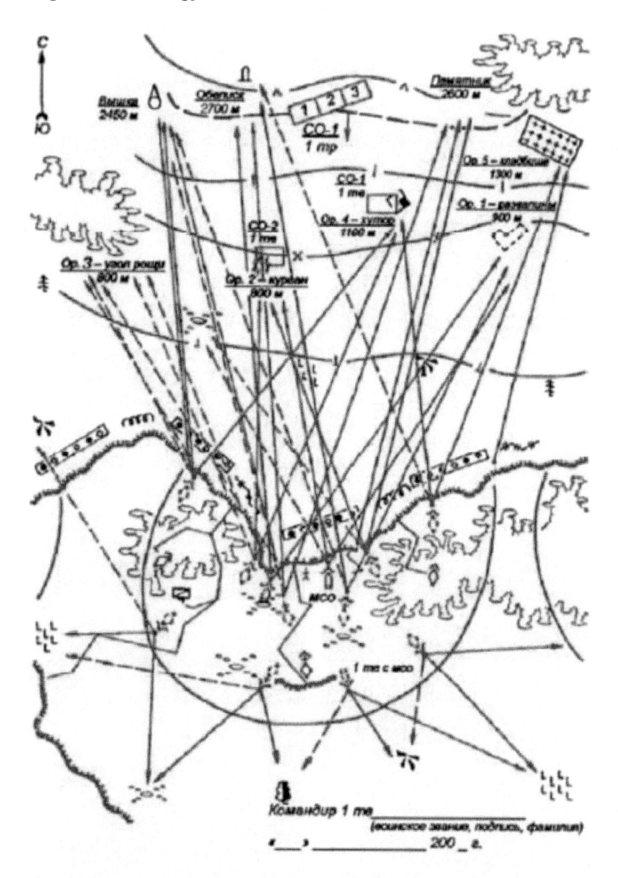

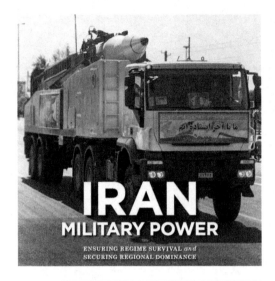

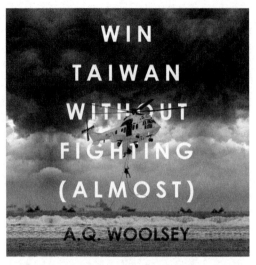

Russian Tank Company Vulnerabilities[2]

It should be noted that Russian battalion tactical groups (BTG) present tactical vulnerabilities that can be exploited by American brigade combat team (BCT) commanders. Shortages in ready maneuver forces, especially infantry, significantly limit Russian maneuver capabilities. BTGs cannot simultaneously mass for offensive operations and maintain flank and rear security, and they struggle to concentrate artillery against attacks on multiple simultaneous axes.

American BCT commanders can maneuver against Russian BTGs' vulnerabilities by avoiding static deployments of forces that allow the BTG commander to select, prepare and execute limited strikes. BTG capabilities are extremely lethal when concentrated against individual units but diminish rapidly against high-tempo distributed maneuver or defense-in-depth because a BTG can't resource economy-of-force missions. In contrast, American BCTs have asymmetrical advantages in maneuver and sustainment, which can be leveraged against a BTG. To defeat a BTG, increase uncertainty and shape the battlefield by "burning more calories" to overload the BTG commander's most valuable systems and personnel. Once hostilities are initiated, attack on multiple fronts to destroy his maneuver force, displace his mission command, EW and fires assets, and seize his sustainment area.

BTGs typically strike from behind a proxy guard force because their strategic imperative is to control terrain to shape post-conflict negotiations. When possible, the BTG commander will employ his strike assets to cause casualties, pressuring his opponent to negotiate the settlement, but he must also preserve his own strength because it cannot be regenerated operationally and casualties are strategically expensive.

Although the BTG deploys with a large complement of direct- and general-support units, only a reinforced battalion of maneuver forces are available to the BTG commander. To compensate for the shortage of maneuver forces, and to preserve combat power, BTGs employ a force of local paramilitary units as proxy forces to secure terrain and guard the BTG from direct and indirect attack. These units are comprised of local militia, Russian veteran volunteers and mercenaries who defend the line of contact and key infrastructure.

The guard force is also the source of the BTG's freedom of maneuver – its presence frees up the BTG's maneuver soldiers from security missions, protects them from attack and allows the BTG commander both free movement to his point of attack and time to prepare the battlefield for the attack. When opportunities to strike Ukrainian forces are identified or if the proxies are attacked, the BTG can employ indirect fires from behind the guard force to destroy its adversary with minimal risk to the regular force.

Operations in a BTG physically and geographically center on the group commander. Once the plan is issued, the lack of common operating picture (COP) technology at the platoon level limits the BTG's flexibility and its commander's ability to quickly disseminate enemy updates, change sub-units' orders and communicate with adjacent units. Communications between the BTG and paramilitary forces are particularly tenuous. Paramilitary commanders said they use cellular phones, satellite phones or unencrypted radios to communicate with the BTG headquarters.

---

[2] Defeating the Russian Battalion Tactical Group by CPT Nicolas J. Fiore

The Russian regulars involved in the attack to capture Mariupol in Ukraine were operating without the level of paramilitary support they enjoyed in the eastern parts of Donbass Province. Without these light infantry, even armored forces were unable to overcome the city's defenders. Even the tanks Russia used to support the final approach were only brought up when all other options were exhausted and the separatists had cleared enough of the structures to guarantee the tanks' safety. This is further evidence of tank deployment risk-aversion and over-reliance on artillery and proxy infantry.

Russians rely heavily on artillery and MLRS rockets to bombard an enemy. In an urban environment, forward observers have trouble calling for effective fire and targeting is inaccurate; so, munitions are not as effective against dispersed targets using mass-construction urban terrain as cover. In the battle of Mariupol, a Russian tank battalion was committed to the fight to capture the town, but a company of Ukrainian Army tanks were able to defeat them.

Instead of executing combined-arms maneuver (CAM) to overpower inferior Ukrainian forces, Russian BTGs preferred to escalate contact, employ fires when possible and commit tanks only after thorough reconnaissance. In many ways, BTGs epitomize modern individual vehicle and soldier protection. BTG tanks and BMPs are equipped with multiple active-protection systems and explosive reactive armor, rendering U.S. individual shoulder-fired antitank systems ineffective. The Ukrainian Army reported success using teams of tanks to destroy Russian T-72B3 tanks on several occasions, but multiple hits were required to defeat the T-72B3's second-generation Kontakt-5 explosive reactive armor.

Bear in mind that the criteria for knocking out a tank does not only depend on defeating its armor. It is quite common to simply de-track the tank to disable it, but the tank can still fight albeit from a compromised position. Another effective method of eliminating the combat capability of a tank would be to destroy its observation devices especially the gunner's sights which would prevent the tank from using its weapons.

Ukraine T-72 hit from the front was pushed back by the blast

60

The following report was taken from a 1997 report titled "**Russian-Manufactured Armored Vehicle Vulnerability in Urban Combat: The Chechnya Experience**", by Mr. Lester W. Grau Foreign Military Studies Office, Fort Leavenworth, KS.

In December 1994, the Russian Army entered the breakaway Republic of Chechnya and attempted to seize the Chechen capital of Grozny from the march. After this attempt failed, the Russian Army spent two months in deliberate house-to-house fighting before finally capturing the city. The dispirited Russian conscript force was badly mauled by the more mature, dedicated Chechen force, and the war drags on to this day. During the first month of the conflict, Russian forces wrote off 225 armored vehicles as nonrepairable battle losses. This represents 10.23% of the armored vehicles initially committed to the campaign. The Russians evacuated some of these 225 hulls to the Kubinka test range for analysis. General-Lieutenant A. Galkin, the head of the Armor Directorate, held a conference on their findings on 20 February 1995. The Minister of Defense attended the conference. The results of the conference convinced the Russian Minister of Defense to stop procuring tanks with gas-turbine engines. Further, the analysis disclosed Chechen anti-armor tactics and the vulnerabilities of Russian armored vehicles in urban combat.

CHECHEN ANTI-ARMOR TECHNIQUES

The Chechen forces are armed with Soviet and Russian-produced weapons, and most Chechen fighters served in the Soviet Armed Forces. The Chechen lower-level combat group consists of 15 to 20 personnel subdivided into three or four-man fighting cells. These cells consist of an antitank gunner (normally armed with the RPG-7 or RPG-18 shoulder-fired antitank rocket launcher), a machine gunner and a sniper. Additional personnel serve as ammunition bearers and assistant gunners. Chechen combat groups would deploy these cells as anti-armor hunter-
The linked image cannot be displayed. The file may have been moved, renamed, or deleted. Verify that the link points to the correct file and location.

Killer Teams

The sniper and machine gunner would pin down the supporting infantry while the antitank gunner would engage the armored target. Teams deploy at ground level, in second and third stories, and in basements. Normally five or six hunter-killer teams simultaneously attack a single armored vehicle. Kill shots are generally made against the top, rear and sides of vehicles. Chechens also drop bottles filled with gasoline or jellied fuel on top of vehicles.

The Chechen hunter-killer teams try to trap vehicle columns in city streets where destruction of the first and last vehicles will trap the column and allow its total destruction. The elevation and depression of the Russian main tank guns are incapable of dealing with hunter-killer teams fighting from basements and second or third-story positions and the simultaneous attack from five or six teams negate the effectiveness of the tank's machine guns. The Russians attached ZSU 23-4 and 2S6 track-mounted antiaircraft guns to armored columns to respond to these difficult-to-engage hunter-killer teams.

Initial Russian vehicle losses were due to a combination of inappropriate tactics, underestimation of the opposing force, and a lack of combat readiness. The Russians moved into Grozny without encircling it and sealing it off from reinforcements. They planned to take the city from the march without dismounting. Due to shortages in personnel, the Russian columns consisted of composite units and most personnel carriers traveled with few or no dismounts. These initial columns were decimated.

As the Russians regrouped, they brought in more infantry and began a systematic advance through the city, house by house and block by block. Russian armored vehicle losses dropped off with their change in tactics. Russian infantry moved in front with armored combat vehicles in support or in reserve. Some Russian vehicles were outfitted with a cage of wire mesh mounted some 25-30 centimeters away from the hull armor to defeat the shaped charges of an antitank grenade launcher as well as to protect the vehicle from a Molotov cocktail or bundle of explosives. The Russians began establishing ambushes on approach routes into a selected area and then running vehicles into the area as bait to destroy Chechen hunter-killer teams.

Vulnerabilities Of Russian Armored Vehicles

Shoulder-fired antitank weapons and antitank grenades knocked out the bulk of armored vehicles and each destroyed vehicle took an average of three to six lethal hits. Fuel cells and engines are favorite aiming points for Chechen antitank gunners. The following illustrations have a grey area imposed which shows the area where 90% of the lethal hits occurred.

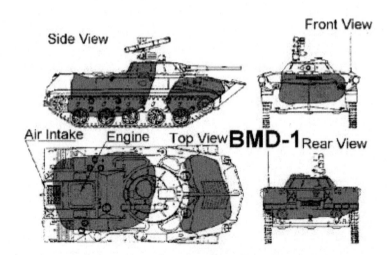

The BMD-1 is a personnel carrier assigned to airborne forces. As such, it is lightly armored. It was vulnerable to front, rear, flanking and top-down fire. The front portion of the turret is reinforced and, consequently, not vulnerable, but the rear of the turret is.

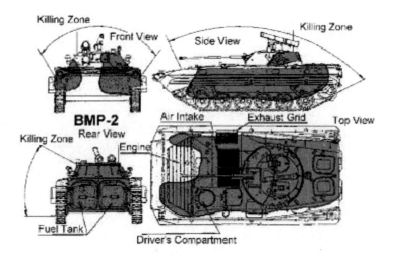

There is more armor on the BMP-2 infantry fighting vehicle. However, its top armor is weak, its fuel tanks are within the rear doors and the driver's compartment is vulnerable.

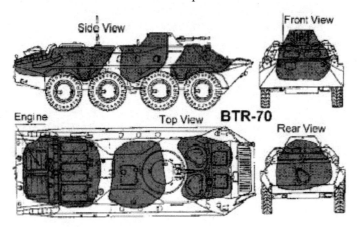

The BTR-70 wheeled armored personnel carrier showed many of the same vulnerabilities as the BMD and BMP.

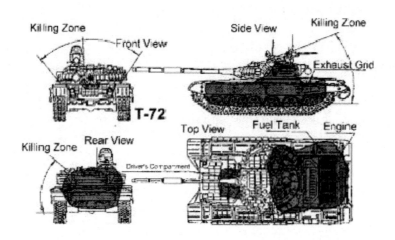

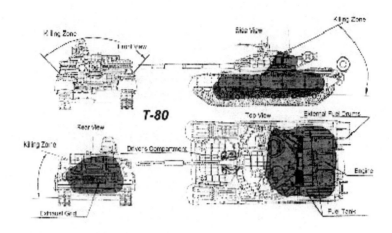

Sixty-two tanks were destroyed in the first month's fighting in Chechnya. Over 98% (apparently 61 tanks) were knocked out by rounds which impacted in areas not protected by reactive armor. The Russians employed the T-72 and T-80 tank in Chechnya. They were both invulnerable to frontal shots, since the front is heavily armored and covered with reactive armor. Kill shots were made at those points where there is no reactive armor--the sides and rear and, on top shots, on the drivers hatch and the rear of the turret and rear deck. Early in the conflict, most Russian tanks went into combat without their reactive armor. They were particularly vulnerable to damaging or lethal frontal hits without it.

CONCLUSIONS

The Chechen forces developed effective techniques to defeat Russian armored vehicles on the streets of a large city. Many of their techniques can be adapted by other armed forces which might fight Russian-manufactured armored vehicles (or other types of armored vehicles) in urban combat. These techniques are:

1. Organize anti-tank hunter-killer teams which include a machine gunner and a sniper to protect the anti-tank gunner by suppressing infantry which is accompanying the armored vehicles.
2. Select anti-armor ambush areas in sections of the city where buildings restrict and canalize the movement of armored vehicles.
3. Lay out the ambush in order to seal off vehicles inside the kill zone.
4. Use multiple hunter-killer teams to engage armored vehicles from basements, ground level and from second- or third-floor positions. A problem with the RPG-7 and RPG-18 antitank weapons are the backblast, signature and time lapse between shots. The Chechens solved the time lapse problem by engaging each target simultaneously with five or six anti-tank weapons (obvious requirements for a future anti-armor weapon for urban combat is a low-signature, multi-shot, recoil-attenuated, light-weight weapon which can be fired from inside enclosures. The AT-4 and Javelin do not appear to meet these requirements).
5. Engage armored targets from the top, rear and sides. Shots against frontal armor protected by reactive armor only serve to expose the gunner.
6. Engage accompanying air-defense guns first.

Russian Tank Commander's Sketch of a Defensive Position

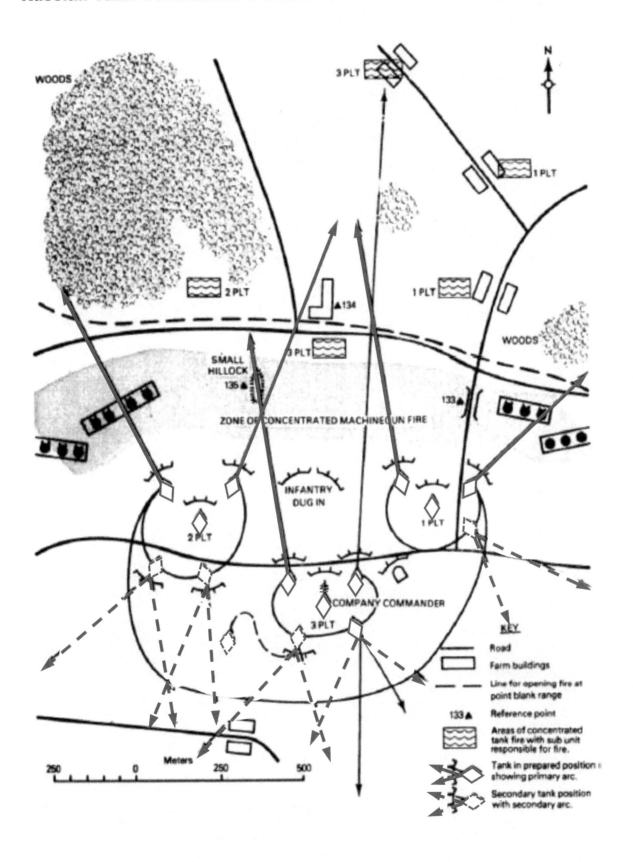

WOODS

3 PLT

1 PLT

2 PLT

1 PLT

▲134

SMALL
HILLOCK
135 ▲

3 PLT

WOODS

133 ▲

ZONE OF CONCENTRATED MACHINEGUN FIRE

INFANTRY
DUG IN

2 PLT

1 PLT

COMPANY COMMANDER

3 PLT

250   0   Meters   250   500

KEY

▬▬▬▬	Road
▭	Farm buildings
─ ─ ─	Line for opening fire at point blank range
133 ▲	Reference point
▨	Areas of concentrated tank fire with sub unit responsible for fire.
	Tank in prepared position : showing primary arc.
	Secondary tank position with secondary arc.

61

Tank Fire Card

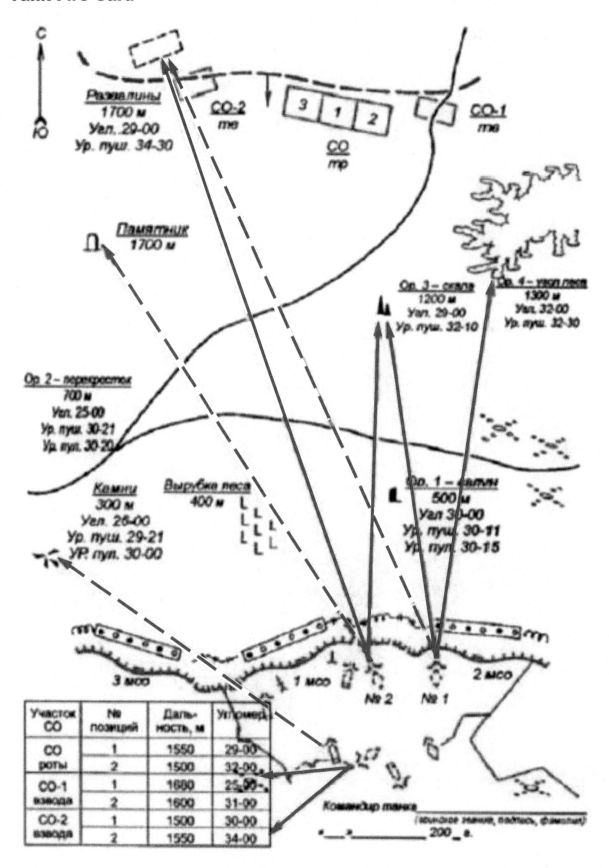

Russian Tank Company Maneuvers
River Crossing Control/Organization

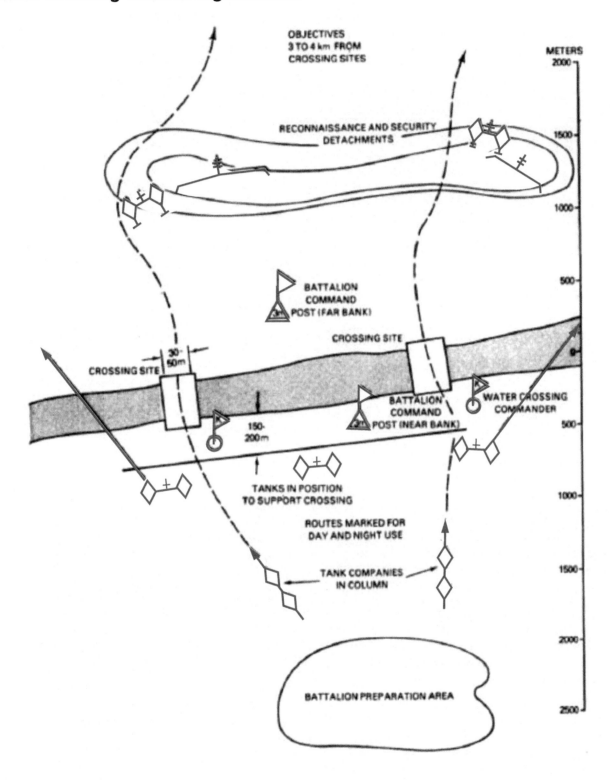

Enveloping Attack by a Reinforced Tank Company

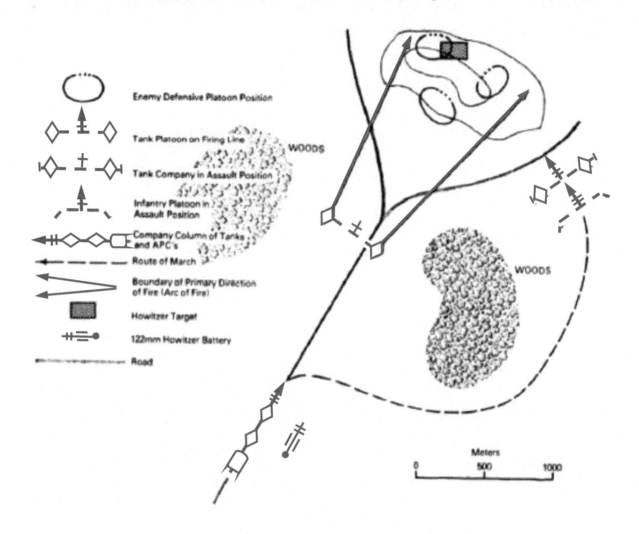

A tank company or platoon in the offensive is assigned an object of attack and the direction of the further offensive. In some cases, when in front of the offensive, the enemy is not reconnoitered, when setting a combat mission by radio, as well as when offensive in special conditions, the platoon can only be pointed in the direction of further offensive. The platoon advances at the front up to 300 m. The object of the tank platoon is usually an observed live force in trenches or other fortifications, as well as tanks, guns, anti-tank missile systems, machine guns and other enemy fire weapons, located in the first trench and in the nearest depth of its defense. The battle formation of a tank platoon usually includes motorized rifle squads, control and fire support group. In addition, the platoon can create group of combat vehicles. Motorized rifle squads, depending on the mission being performed and the conditions of the situation step in a line, with an angle back or with a ledge (to the right or to the left). Intervals between squad along the front and in depth can be up to 50 m. The intervals between tanks can be up to 100 m. A motorized rifle platoon can advance on foot (on skis in winter), on infantry fighting vehicles or landing troops on tanks.

Advance from A Holding Area

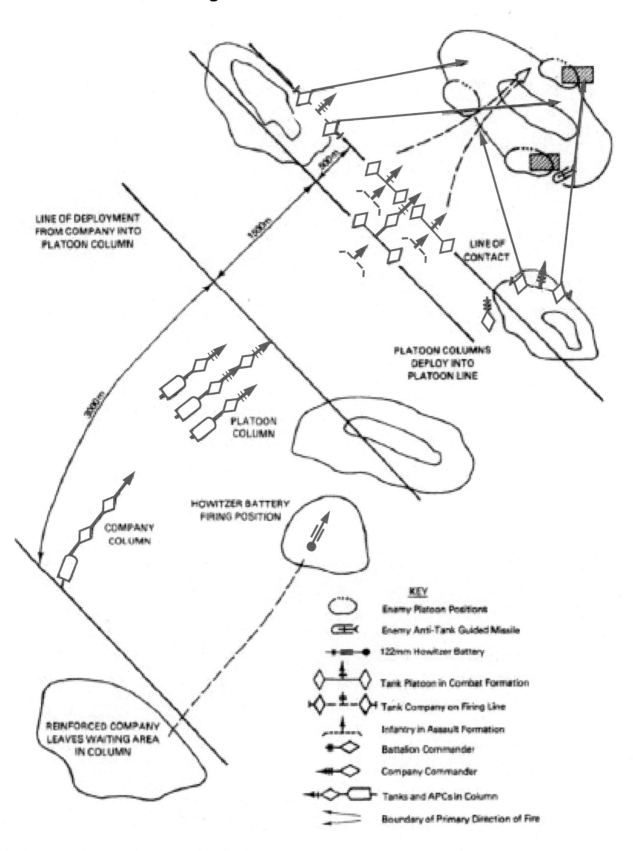

LINE OF DEPLOYMENT
FROM COMPANY INTO
PLATOON COLUMN

LINE OF
CONTACT

PLATOON COLUMNS
DEPLOY INTO
PLATOON LINE

PLATOON
COLUMN

HOWITZER BATTERY
FIRING POSITION

COMPANY
COLUMN

REINFORCED COMPANY
LEAVES WAITING AREA
IN COLUMN

KEY

Enemy Platoon Positions

Enemy Anti-Tank Guided Missile

122mm Howitzer Battery

Tank Platoon in Combat Formation

Tank Company on Firing Line

Infantry in Assault Formation

Battalion Commander

Company Commander

Tanks and APCs in Column

Boundary of Primary Direction of Fire

Assault Formations

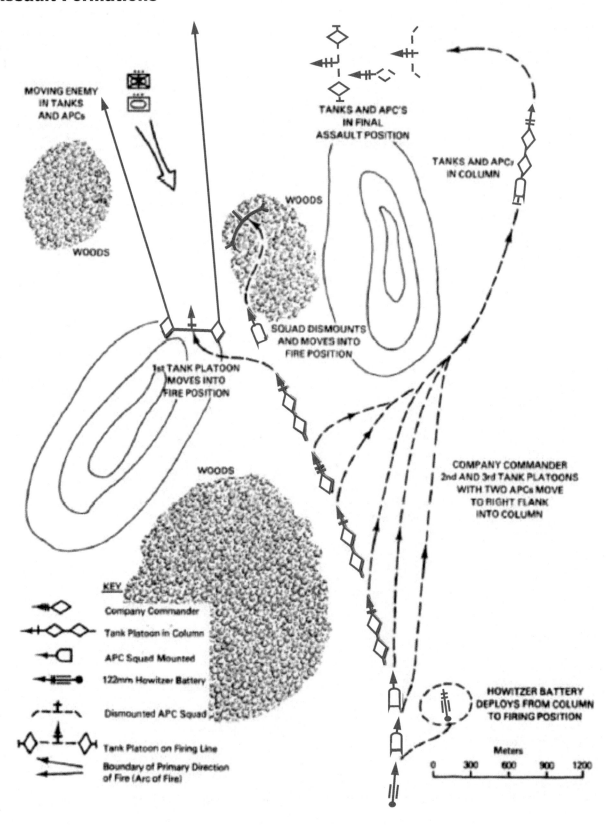

MOVING ENEMY IN TANKS AND APCs

WOODS

TANKS AND APC'S IN FINAL ASSAULT POSITION

TANKS AND APCs IN COLUMN

WOODS

1st TANK PLATOON MOVES INTO FIRE POSITION

SQUAD DISMOUNTS AND MOVES INTO FIRE POSITION

WOODS

COMPANY COMMANDER 2nd AND 3rd TANK PLATOONS WITH TWO APCs MOVE TO RIGHT FLANK INTO COLUMN

KEY

Company Commander

Tank Platoon in Column

APC Squad Mounted

122mm Howitzer Battery

Dismounted APC Squad

Tank Platoon on Firing Line

Boundary of Primary Direction of Fire (Arc of Fire)

HOWITZER BATTERY DEPLOYS FROM COLUMN TO FIRING POSITION

Meters

0   300   600   900   1200

Breakthrough of the Hasty Defense Position

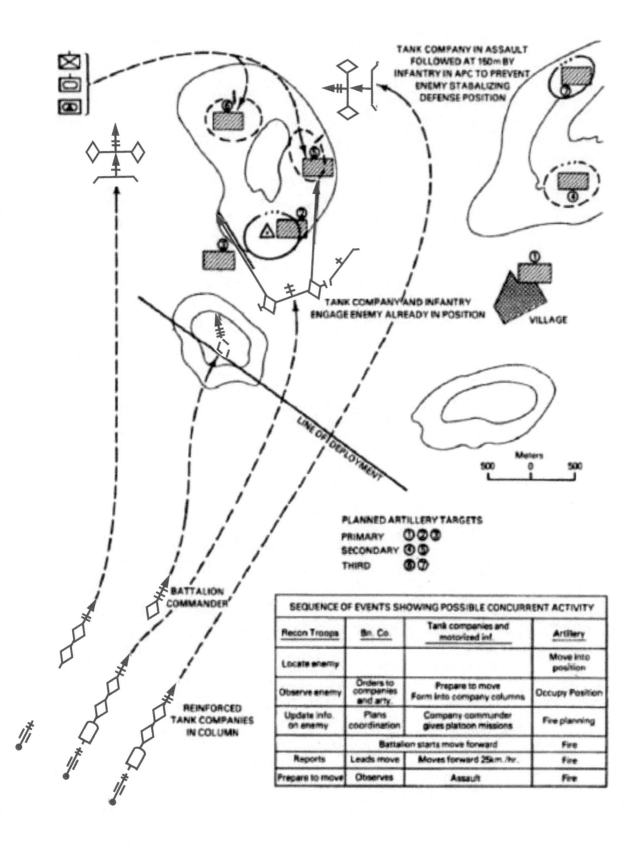

TANK COMPANY IN ASSAULT FOLLOWED AT 150m BY INFANTRY IN APC TO PREVENT ENEMY STABALIZING DEFENSE POSITION

TANK COMPANY AND INFANTRY ENGAGE ENEMY ALREADY IN POSITION

VILLAGE

LINE OF DEPLOYMENT

Meters
500   0   500

BATTALION COMMANDER

REINFORCED TANK COMPANIES IN COLUMN

PLANNED ARTILLERY TARGETS
PRIMARY ①②③
SECONDARY ④⑤
THIRD ⑥⑦

SEQUENCE OF EVENTS SHOWING POSSIBLE CONCURRENT ACTIVITY			
Recon Troops	Bn. Co.	Tank companies and motorized inf.	Artillery
Locate enemy			Move into position
Observe enemy	Orders to companies and arty.	Prepare to move Form into company columns	Occupy Position
Update info. on enemy	Plans coordination	Company commander gives platoon missions	Fire planning
Battalion starts move forward			Fire
Reports	Leads move	Moves forward 25km./hr.	Fire
Prepare to move	Observes	Assault	Fire

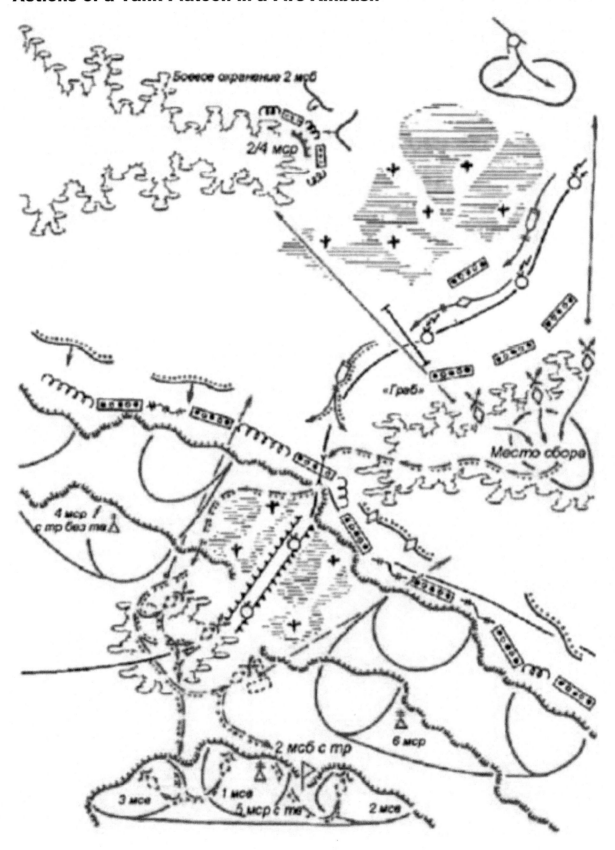

Action of a Motorized Rifle Squad and Tanks in a Village

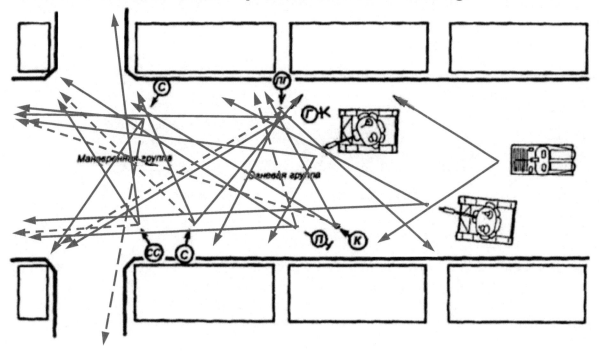

During the offensive when capturing a village, a motorized rifle platoon can operate as part of a motorized rifle company to form the basis assault group. A tank platoon is usually attached to an assault group or acts in conjunction with a motorized rifle unit with a ledge on both side streets behind the battle formations of motorized rifle subunits. Attack movement of the assault group starts simultaneously with the units of the first echelon.

Trench for a Tank for Circular Fire

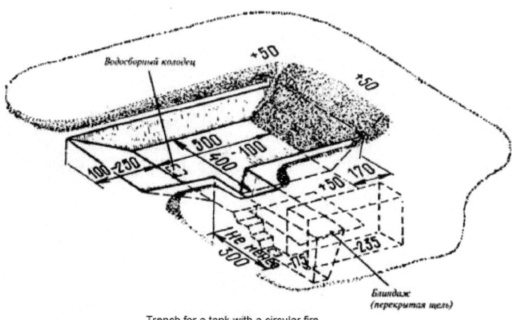

Trench for a tank with a circular fire

Tandem Missile Warheads and Relikt ERA

Tandem Missile Warheads

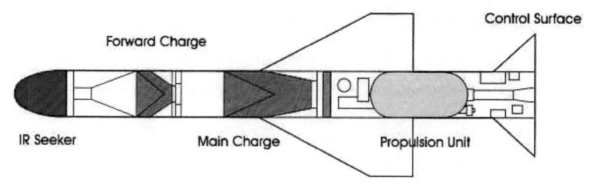

Tandem warhead missiles, are designed to defeat explosive reactive armor (ERA) by detonating it early. A forward charge is a much smaller shaped charge as compared to the main shaped charge. When the tandem missile hits, the forward charge triggers, setting off the explosive in the reactive armor. Once the ERA charge is expended, the main charge can pierce vehicle armor.

Relikt Explosive Reactive Armor (ERA)

Kontakt-5 ERA only sends an outer plate outwards at an angle. The movement of the plate disrupts the movement and formation of the metallic jet generated by the shaped charge, degrading its performance. *Relikt ERA* works a little differently with the explosive layer comprised of several shaped charges. The shaped charges within the armor are built as channels, essentially forming blades of molten metal that fly out in combination with the top plate. These blades also appear to trigger in sequence, with the channels closest to the one damaged popping first.

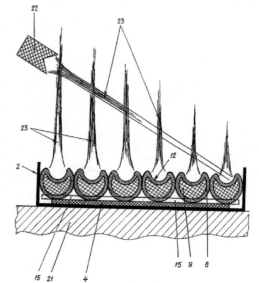

This delay means that, in all probability, the missiles main charge will be in position to get sliced apart before it can detonate. Shaped charge warheads are also delicate items. There's very little actual explosive charge, with the penetration instead being dependent on how well the explosive can actually shape the molten penetrator. Slicing the main charge and its metallic liner into two or more sections renders it substantially less effective. This also has the benefit of being really effective against sabots, as the sabot is sliced apart, rendering it a fraction of the threat it initially posed.

Relikt ERA

Note the difference in Relikt ERA on the Russian **T-80BVM** (see below). The back side of the ERA boxes have one additional module. The standart Relikt doesn't have this module.

Kontakt-5 (2nd generation) ERA

Other books we publish on Amazon.com

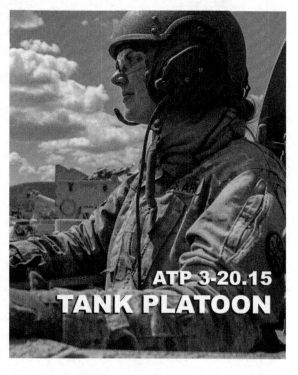

Printed in Great Britain
by Amazon

17210193R10052